The
LIBERTY CODE

TYLER GILREATH

The

LIBERTY CODE

HOW THE FOUNDERS' SECRET WRITINGS EXPOSE
THE UFO AGENDA AND THE COMING ALIEN CRISIS

DEFENDER

CRANE, MO

The Liberty Code: How the Founders' Secret Writings Expose the UFO Agenda and the Coming Alien Crisis

By Tyler Gilreath

Defender Publishing
Crane, MO 65633

©2025 Defender Publishing

All Rights Reserved. Published 2024

ISBN: 9781948014908

Printed in the United States of America.

A CIP catalog record of this book is available from the Library of Congress.

Cover designer: Dakota Jackson
Interior designer: Katherine Lloyd

For my loving wife and children,
whose constant support fuels my exploration
of the unknown and unexplained.
Without your unwavering encouragement and God's guidance,
this book would not have been possible.

CONTENTS

PREFACE

T he church and the concept of extraterrestrial life have always been
uneasy companions. Now, with governments, scientists, and aca-
demia taking the subject seriously, Christians can no longer afford to
remain on the sidelines, silent and unengaged.

I have dedicated my life to exploring the realms of high strangeness
and the supernatural. In my previous works—*Gospel Over Gods: Jesus
Christ, the Fallen Angels, and the Supernatural War of the Bible* and *Gate
of the Gods: Revelation, the Messiah, and the Second Coming of Babylon*—I
delved into the hidden and often terrifying aspects of our world and the
supernatural realm. This book continues that journey, seeking out truths
that challenge conventional beliefs.

My goal with this book is to conduct a historical and theological
investigation into the UFO (unidentified flying object) phenomenon
and the implications it holds for humanity. My research has led me to
believe we are on the brink of a disclosure that could alter life as we
know it. The reality of extraterrestrial intelligence raises profound questions and presents potential challenges to faith. Many Christians may
find themselves unprepared for such an earth-shattering revelation, and
this book aims to provide the context and understanding necessary to
navigate these uncharted waters.

I recognize that this book may provoke cognitive dissonance, challenging deeply held beliefs and prompting serious reflection. However,
my hope is that it equips readers with the tools to critically investigate
and discern the true nature of the UFO phenomenon. As we navigate
these complexities, we must remain vigilant and open to the possibility

that not everything is as it appears. The phenomenon may signify a deeper, more insidious deception, making it essential to understand the spiritual context and the insights of the Founding Fathers to unravel this mystery.

Introduction

COSMIC REVELATIONS:
UNVEILING HIDDEN TRUTHS
IN THE HALLS OF POWER

The Revelation

On the morning of July 26, 2023, the air inside the Rayburn House Office Building in Washington, DC, crackled with anticipation. At 10:00 a.m., the House Committee on Oversight and Accountability was set to convene a hearing unlike any before it. Representatives, aides, and a select group of military and intelligence insiders filed into the chamber, their expressions betraying the gravity of what was to come. All eyes were on the three men seated behind the long table—Ryan Graves, David Grusch, and Commander David Fravor. These were not ordinary witnesses; they were bearers of extraordinary experiences that defied logic, men whose testimonies would challenge everything the world thought it knew.

As the chairman's gavel struck, the atmosphere grew tense, charged with the weight of impending revelations. All eyes turned to Ryan Graves, the former Navy pilot, as he began:

My name is Ryan "FOBS" Graves and I am a former F–18 pilot with a decade of service in the U.S. Navy including two deployments in Operation Enduring Freedom and Operation Inherent Resolve. I have experienced advanced UAP [unidentified aerial phenomena] firsthand and I am here to voice the concerns of more than 30 commercial aircrew and military veterans who have confided their similar encounters with me.[1]

He quickly brought attention to the obstacles faced by those reporting UAP encounters:

The stigma attached to UAP is real and powerful and challenges national security. It silences commercial pilots who fear professional repercussions, discourages witnesses, and is only compounded by recent government claims questioning the credibility of eyewitness testimony. Parts of our government are aware more about UAP than they let on, but excessive classification practices keep crucial information hidden. Since 2021 all UAP videos are classified as secret or above. This level of secrecy not only impedes our understanding but fuels speculation and mistrust.[2]

Graves then recounted to the captivated officials his 2014 experience as an F–18 pilot with the Red Rippers:

In 2014, I was an F–18 Foxtrot pilot in the Navy Fighter Attack Squadron 11, the Red Rippers, and I was stationed at NAS Oceana in Virginia Beach. After upgrades were made to our jet's radar systems, we began detecting unknown objects operating in our airspace. At first, we assumed they were radar errors but soon we began to correlate the radar tracks with multiple onboard sensors, including infrared systems, eventually through visual ID.

During a training mission in Warning Area W–72, 10 miles off the coast of Virginia Beach, two F–18 Super Hornets were

2

split by a UAP. The object, described as a dark gray or a black cube inside of a clear sphere, came within 50 feet of the lead aircraft and was estimated to be five to 15 feet in diameter. The mission commander terminated the flight immediately and returned to base. Our squadron submitted a safety report but there was no official acknowledgement of the incident and no further mechanism to report the sightings. Soon these encounters became so frequent that aircrew would discuss the risk of UAP as part of their regular preflight briefs.[3]

Graves didn't stop at describing incidents. He explained the broader implications and a need for action. Recognizing the need for action and answers, he founded *Americans for Safe Aerospace*." He said:

The organization has since become a haven for UAP witnesses who were previously unspoken due to the absence of a safe intake process. More than thirty witnesses have come forward and almost 5,000 Americans have joined us in the fight for transparency at safeaerospace.org.

The majority of witnesses are commercial pilots at major airlines. Often, they are veterans with decades of flying experience. Pilots are reporting UAP at altitudes that appear above them at 40,000 feet, potentially in low Earth orbit or in the gray zone below the common line, making unexplainable maneuvers like right hand turns and retrograde orbits, or J hooks.[4]

The testimonies of other pilots corroborated his account, with frequent reports of objects making unexplainable maneuvers. As Graves concluded, the message was clear: "I believe these accounts are only scratching the surface and more will share their experiences once it is safe to do so."[5]

Graves' testimony struck a nerve with the committee. Here was a man who had not only seen these objects with his own eyes, but who had also flown missions that brought him dangerously close to them. His voice carried the weight of personal experience—a professional who had faced the unknown and lived to tell the tale.

As Graves spoke, the committee members shifted in their seats, the gravity of the situation becoming more apparent with each word. The objects Graves described weren't just potential threats—they were ongoing risks to both military and civilian aircraft.

"The American people deserve to know what is happening in our skies," he concluded. "It is long overdue.[6]

Next, the chairman turned to David Grusch, the former intelligence officer who had become a whistleblower, risking his career to expose what he believed to be a decades-long cover-up. Grusch's testimony was less about a single event and more about a pattern—a deeply entrenched secrecy within the government regarding unidentified aerial phenomena (UAPs).

My name is David Charles Grusch. I was an intelligence officer for 14 years both in the U.S. Air Force, both active-duty Air National Guard and Reserve at the rank of Major and most recently from 2021 to 2023—at the National Geospatial Intelligence Agency, NGA, at the GS–15 civilian level, which is the military equivalent of a full bird colonel.

Everyone in the room listened intently, the gravity of his position giving weight to his words.

I became a whistleblower through a PPD–19 urgent concern filing in May 2022 with the intelligence community inspector general following concerning reports from multiple esteemed and credentialed current and former military and intelligence community individuals that the U.S. Government is operating with secrecy above congressional oversight with regards to UAPs (i.e., UFOs).

My testimony is based on information I have been given by individuals with a long-standing track record of legitimacy

4

and service to this country, many of whom also have shared compelling evidence in the form of photography, official documentation, and classified oral testimony to myself and many of my various colleagues.

Grusch then elaborated on the lengths to which he had gone to verify his sources:

I have taken every step I can to corroborate this evidence over a period of 4 years while I was with the UAP Task Force and do my due diligence on the individuals sharing it. It is because of these steps, I believe strongly in the importance of bringing this information before you.

His voice grew firmer as he invoked a sense of duty:

I am driven by a commitment…to truth and transparency, rooted in our inherent duty to uphold the United States Constitution and protect the American people. I am asking Congress to hold our government to this standard and thoroughly investigate these claims.

But as I stand here under oath now, I am speaking to the facts as I have been told them. In the U.S. Air Force in my National Reconnaissance Office—NRO—reservist capacity, I was a member of the UAP Task Force from 2019 to 2021….

In 2019, the UAP Task Force Director asked me to identify all special access programs and controlled access programs, also known as SAPs…. I was informed in the course of my official duties of a multi-decade UAP crash retrieval and reverse engineering program to which I was denied access to those additional read-ons when I requested it.[7]

A murmur ran through the room. Grusch's statements were both shocking and, for some, confirmation of long-held suspicions. He spoke of colleagues who had come forward with similar accounts, of programs hidden deep within the bureaucracy that operated without oversight, and of materials and technologies that couldn't be explained by any known science.

> I made the decision based on the data I collected to report this information to my superiors and multiple inspectors general... in effect, becoming a whistleblower. As you know, I have suffered retaliation for my decision, but I am hopeful that my actions will ultimately lead to a positive outcome of increased transparency.[8]

The chairman's eyes narrowed slightly as he processed Grusch's words. The implications were staggering. If what Grusch claimed was true, the government had been sitting on potentially world-altering technologies, keeping them hidden from the public and its elected representatives. The trust between the governed and those in power hung in the balance.

Finally, it was Commander David Fravor's turn. A retired Navy pilot with decades of experience, Fravor's presence commanded the room. He began with the now-infamous "Tic Tac" encounter off the coast of California in 2004, an event that had already become legendary among those in the know.

> My name is David Fravor. I am a retired Commander in the United States Navy. In 2004, I was a commanding officer of Strike Fighter Squadron 41, the world-famous Black Aces. We were tasked to Carrier Airwing 11 stationed on board the USS Nimitz and had begun a 2-month workup cycle off the coast of California.[9]

As Fravor recounted the encounter, the weight of his experience lent profound credibility to the story. The room seemed to grow still, the committee members hanging on his every word as he described how the training exercise suddenly transformed into a real-world tasking.

When we launched off, Nimitz, my wingman was joining up.…
We were told that the training was going to be suspended and we
[were] going to proceed with real-world tasking.[10]

Fravor's account grew more intense as he described the sighting. It
wasn't just another unknown blip on the radar; it was something alto-
gether different—something alive, as if it was responding to their presence.

There the controller told us that these objects had been observed
for over 2 weeks coming down from over 80,000 feet, rapidly
descending to 20,000 feet, hanging out for hours, and then
going straight back up. For those that do not realize, above
80,000 feet is space. There were no rotors, no rotor wash, or any
sign of visible control surfaces like wings.[11]

The implications of Fravor's words rippled through those in the
chamber. The impossibility of what he described wasn't lost on anyone:
a tic-tac shaped object that defied known physics, maneuvering in ways
no human-engineered craft could replicate.

Our altitude at this point was about 15,000 feet and a Tic Tac was
about 12,000. As we pulled nose onto the object within about a
half mile of it, it rapidly accelerated in front of us and disappeared.[12]

Fravor's voice remained steady, but the tension in the room was palpable. He had just described an object that could outmaneuver anything
in their fleet, vanishing in a way that defied all logic and technology. It
wasn't simply evasive, it was untouchable.
He then shifted his tone to address the larger implications:

What concerns me is that there is no oversight from our elected
officials on anything associated with our government processing
or working on craft believed not from this world.[13]

The room grew quiet as Fravor emphasized the urgency of the matter. The problem wasn't only the encounters themselves, but the lack of transparency surrounding them.

This issue is not a full public disclosure that can undermine national security, but it is about ensuring that our system of checks and balances works across all work done in the government using taxpayer funds.[14]

Fravor's appeal wasn't just about unveiling secrets; it was about accountability—a call for proper governance over whatever truths were being hidden from the public.

In closing, I would like to say that the Tic Tac object we engaged in 2004 was far superior to anything that we had one time, have today, or [are] looking to develop in the next 10 years.[15]

As Fravor recounted his experience, the committee members leaned in, captivated by his account. His description of the object's impossible movements—darting from one point to another with no visible means of propulsion—left them grappling with the implications. This was no mere glitch in radar systems or a misidentified conventional aircraft. This was something far more advanced.

The chairman's face was inscrutable as he listened, but the gravity of the testimony wasn't lost on him. Fravor's calm, measured delivery only heightened the impact of his words. This was a seasoned pilot, a man whose word carried the weight of experience and credibility, and he was describing something that should not exist.

As the hearing continued, the questions from the committee grew more pointed. The members pressed for details, seeking to understand not only the technical aspects of the phenomena, but also the broader implications. How long had this been happening? Why had it been kept secret for so long? What did this mean for national security?

Graves, Grusch, and Fravor responded with the clarity and serious-ness the situation demanded. They spoke of radar systems that were jammed, of flight maneuvers no human pilot could survive, and of the psychological toll such encounters had on those who experienced them.

It was a session unlike any other—a rare moment of bipartisan agreement on the need for greater transparency and oversight when it came to UAPs. The hearing ended with a sense of urgency, of a mission only just beginning. The testimonies of Graves, Grusch, and Fravor had opened a door that could not be closed, a door that led to a future where the mysteries of the skies might finally be unraveled.

As the three men left the hearing room, they knew their journey was far from over. The revelations they had shared were just the tip of the iceberg. What lay beneath—buried in classified reports and hidden pro-grams—would take years, perhaps decades, to fully uncover. But they were committed to the task, driven by a shared belief that the truth, no matter how unsettling, was worth pursuing.

The committee members, too, were left to ponder the implications of what they had heard. The next steps would be critical—legislation, oversight, international cooperation—all necessary to ensure that the mysteries of the skies were no longer shrouded in secrecy. The world had changed in that hearing room, and there was no going back.

Conclusion

As more government officials come forward and belief in extraterrestrial life continues to grow, the Church must confront these emerging pos-sibilities and discern the true nature and intentions of these purported visitors. What if "aliens" do exist? How would that alter your percep-tion of the world and reality? And what if these beings are not visitors from distant planets, but demons from the very depths of darkness? If so, shouldn't Christians be the ones sounding the alarm? This study is designed to bring the alien manifesto out of the shadows.

In this historical and theological investigation, we will venture into uncharted territories, both in history and understanding. The truths we're about to uncover are far more unsettling than you may anticipate. Perhaps the most vivid example of this lies in the early years of the United States, where the Founding Fathers wrestled with the possibility of life from other worlds. As we explore their thoughts and fears, you may find striking parallels to our own uncertainties today—but what they uncovered might shock you.

Chapter 1

THE INAUGURAL PRESIDENT
AND THE INHABITANTS OF OTHER WORLDS

> It is yet to be decided whether the Revolution must ulti-
> mately be considered as a blessing or a curse: a blessing or
> a curse, not to the present age alone, for with our fate will
> the destiny of unborn millions be involved.
>
> —GEORGE WASHINGTON

On December 17, 1796, the chill of the December air settled like a shroud over Philadelphia. George Washington, the esteemed president of the young United States, sat in contemplation within the First Presbyterian Church on High Street at noon. The soft murmur of hushed conversations floated around him, but his thoughts were elsewhere, drifting back to the turbulent days of the Revolutionary War. It was in such moments of solemn reflection that he often pondered the fragility of life and the inexorable march of death. Washington's eyes settled on the black-draped, empty coffin at the front of the church. David Rittenhouse, one of the most brilliant minds of their era, was dead.

Rittenhouse had departed this life on June 26, leaving a profound void in the scientific community. His mastery of astronomy, highlighted by the 1769 transit of Venus, marked a turning point in American science. As president of the American Philosophical Society, he advanced knowledge and embodied the nation's intellectual spirit. His precision instruments set lasting standards, and his leadership bridged reason with the ideals of the fledgling nation. In both life and death, Rittenhouse inspired a path toward enlightenment.

The memorial address was a grand affair, attended by not only the members of the American Philosophical Society, but also by members of the Senate and House of Representatives, foreign dignitaries, and a host of notable figures from across the country. The flickering candlelight cast long shadows across the solemn faces, reflecting the gravity of the occasion. Washington himself had been formally invited by the Society, a testament to the high regard in which Rittenhouse was held.[16]

As the eulogium began, delivered by the renowned Dr. Benjamin Rush, a signer of the Declaration of Independence, Washington's mind would have wandered to his own interactions with Rittenhouse. Their acquaintance likely began in the fall of 1774 when Washington attended the First Continental Congress in Philadelphia. The precise instruments crafted by Rittenhouse and his work on surveying colonial boundaries caught Washington's attention.

In June 1779, Washington had written to Rittenhouse seeking his expertise to repair a theodolite—a precision instrument for measuring angles in surveying.[17] As Washington oversaw the nation's expansion, accurate land surveys were crucial, and only a craftsman of Rittenhouse's caliber could be trusted with such a vital task. Later, in 1792, Washington appointed Rittenhouse as the first director of the United States Mint, recognizing his unparalleled integrity and competence. Letters exchanged between Washington, Rittenhouse, Thomas Jefferson, and Alexander Hamilton regarding the mint's operations and finances underscored a mutual respect that transcended their formal roles.

Dr. Rush's voice echoed through the church, recounting Rittenhouse's life and achievements. "We are assembled this day upon a mournful occasion," Dr. Rush said. "Death has made an inroad upon our Society. Our illustrious and beloved President, David Rittenhouse, is no more."[18]

The mourners listened intently as Rush painted a vivid picture of Rittenhouse's humble beginnings in Germantown, his self-taught mastery of mathematics and clock-making, and his groundbreaking construction of an orrery that modeled the solar system with unprecedented accuracy. Washington remembered how Rittenhouse's meticulous craftsmanship had even extended to creating his own reading glasses, a personal favor that exemplified Rittenhouse's generosity and skill.

But it was when Rush began to quote Rittenhouse's thoughts on the cosmos that Washington was jolted from his reverie. Rush read:

How far the inhabitants of other planets may resemble man, we cannot pretend to say. If like them they were created liable to fall, yet some, if not all of them, may still retain their original rectitude. We will hope they do; the thought is comfortable.[19]

Washington undoubtedly felt a stirring within him, a reminder of the vast unknown that Rittenhouse had so passionately explored. The commemoration continued, weaving together the threads of Rittenhouse's scientific inquiries with his deep philosophical and theological reflections. It was clear that Rittenhouse saw the study of the heavens not merely as a pursuit of knowledge, but as a way to understand the divine order and humanity's place within it.

Rush's voice grew more impassioned as he delved into Rittenhouse's visionary musings.

Cease then Galileo to improve thy optic tube, and thou great Newton, forbear thy ardent search into the mysteries of nature, lest ye make unwelcome discoveries. Deprive us not of the pleasure of believing that yonder orbs, traversing in silent majesty the ethereal regions, are the peaceful seats of innocence and bliss, where neither natural nor moral evil has ever intruded, and where to enjoy with gratitude and adoration the Creator's bounty, is the business of existence.[20]

The congregation was rapt, their imaginations ignited by the possibility that the stars above might harbor other forms of life, untouched by the strife and corruption of Earth. Washington, too, likely felt his mind expand with the contemplation of such celestial mysteries.

Rush continued:

If their inhabitants resemble man in their faculties and affections, let us suppose that they are wise enough to govern themselves according to the dictates of that reason God has given, in such a manner as to consult their own, and each other's happiness upon all occasions. But if on the contrary, they have found it necessary to erect artificial fabrics of government, let us not suppose they have done it with so little skill, and at such an enormous expense, as to render them a misfortune instead of a blessing. We will hope that their statesmen are patriots, and that their kings (if that order of beings has found admittance there) have the feelings of humanity. Happy people! And perhaps more happy still, that all communication with us is denied. We have neither corrupted you with our vices, nor injured you by violence. None of your sons and daughters have been degraded from their native dignity, and doomed to endless slavery in America, merely because their bodies may be disposed to reflect, or absorb the rays of light different from ours. Even you, inhabitants of the Moon, situated in our very neighbourhood, are effectually secured from the rapacious hands of the oppressors of our globe.[21]

Washington pondered these words, reflecting on the young republic he led and the principles of self-governance and reason that underpinned it. The notion that other worlds might achieve what humanity on Earth struggled to perfect was both humbling and inspiring.

As the service drew to a close, Rush told the esteemed company of Rittenhouse:

> Agreeably to his request, his body was interred in his observatory near his dwelling house, in the presence of a numerous concourse of his fellow-citizens. It was natural for him in the near prospect of appearing in the presence of his Maker, to feel an attachment to that spot in which he had cultivated a knowledge of his perfections, and held communion with him through the medium of his works. Hereafter it shall become one of the objects of curiosity in our city. Thither shall the philosophers of future ages resort to do homage to his tomb, and children yet unborn, shall point to the dome which covers it, and exultingly say, "there lies our Rittenhouse. Let us my respected colleagues, repair for a few minutes to that awful spot."[22]

Washington joined the solemn procession leading to David Rittenhouse's final resting place, an observatory near his home where he had spent countless nights unraveling the mysteries of the universe. It was a fitting tribute to a man whose life's work had been to illuminate cosmic enigmas.

The telescope, once a tool of discovery in Rittenhouse's hands, now stood silent, pointed earthward as if in mourning. The simplicity of the tombstone, bearing only his name and the dates of his birth and death, spoke volumes of his modesty. Washington and the company of patriots paused at the tombstone, reflecting on the loss of a friend, a scientist, and an American whose contributions would continue to inspire generations to come.

One can wonder if Washington, before retiring to his home, lingered a moment longer, his thoughts still entwined with the stirring words of Benjamin Rush. Did the possibility of life on other worlds ignite his imagination and kindle a sense of unease?

Turning away from the grave, Washington walked slowly towards his carriage. The crisp winter air nipped at his face, yet his thoughts were far from the cold. Did the idea that the stars above might harbor other beings untouched by human flaws fill him with both awe and trepidation? Could Rittenhouse's words, echoed by Rush—"Cease then Galileo to improve thy optic tube, and thou great Newton, forbear thy ardent search into the mysteries of nature, lest ye make unwelcome discoveries"—reverberate in his mind, warning him of the potential dangers celestial discoveries might unveil? Might the weight of leadership have felt heavier with the realization that humanity's grasp of the cosmos was still so limited? How would a president, a leader bound to the Earth and its immediate struggles, deal with a force from beyond the stars?

The carriage jolted into motion, and Washington stared out the window at the bustling streets of Philadelphia. The snow-dusted cobblestones glistened under the pale winter sun, and the breath of passersby formed fleeting clouds in the crisp air. He knew the nation's strength was rooted in its unity and its pursuit of knowledge. Perhaps, he mused, the key to facing any potential presence among the stars lay in the very principles that had founded the United States: reason, courage, and a steadfast commitment to the common good. Did he resolve that the nation must continue to foster its scientific pursuits, to support minds like Rittenhouse's who could navigate the stars and uncover their secrets?

As the carriage ferried him away from the corpse of Rittenhouse, Washington's mind must have been a swirl of thoughts. The future was uncertain, and the universe vast and mysterious. Yet, he felt a flicker of confidence that with wisdom, unity, and the spirit of discovery, the nation could face whatever challenges were ahead—even those from the stars.

"Rest well, my friend," Washington may have inwardly pledged. The legacy of the great philosopher and astronomer would guide him—and future presidents—illuminating the path through the unknown as he steered the young republic toward a future that embraced the heavens above and the Earth below.

Looking Ahead

As George Washington's carriage moved away from the observatory where David Rittenhouse now rested, his thoughts remained with the vastness of the heavens. The weight of Rittenhouse's musings on life beyond Earth lingered in his mind, perhaps unsettling, but also inspiring. Washington, ever the man of action, knew his role was to lead his young nation through the challenges of this world. Yet, he couldn't help but wonder: What if there were greater challenges out there, waiting just beyond the stars?

But Washington would not face these questions alone. In the months to come, the philosophical weight of the cosmos would be passed to his vice president, John Adams. Adams, a man equally devoted to reason and inquiry, would soon take the mantle of leadership and steer the nation through uncertain waters. But unlike Washington, Adams' gaze was often cast upwards, beyond the immediate struggles of nation-building and toward the mysteries of the universe. His diaries, filled with contemplations on the nature of otherworldly beings, revealed a mind eager to grapple with the larger questions of existence.

As Washington's chapter closed, the nation turned toward Adams—a leader not just of a new republic, but of a new era of thought. What would Adams' speculations reveal about the place of humanity within the cosmic order? Would his reflections challenge the very beliefs upon which the nation was built? The questions loomed large, just as they did for Washington.

And so, the story continues—into the mind of a philosopher-president, where the inhabitants of other worlds weren't just a distant possibility, but a tantalizing reality.

THE PHILOSOPHICAL PRESIDENT
AND THE EXTRATERRESTRIAL DIARIES

For I believe that...the INFINITE has created many
beings...with a beautiful and admirable System of Planets.

—BENJAMIN FRANKLIN

The Diary of John Adams

In the months following Rittenhouse's funeral, the philosophical musings and scientific speculations of the late astronomer likely lingered in the minds of many, including the nation's top leaders. President George Washington and Vice President John Adams, who would soon succeed Washington as president, had time to reflect on Rittenhouse's intriguing comments about life on other planets.

Adams, a thinker deeply engaged with the vastness of the cosmos, had written extensively on such matters in his youth. His diary from 1756 revealed a mind captivated by the possibilities of an infinite universe filled with rational beings. He pondered the capabilities of human understanding, contemplating the enlargement of the mind to comprehend the whole created universe and its inhabitants. Adams wrote:

We find ourselves capable of comprehending many Things, of acquiring considerable Degrees of Knowledge by our slender and contracted Faculties. Now may we not suppose our minds strengthened, and Capacities dilated, so as fully to comprehend this Globe of Earth, with its numerous appendages? May we not suppose them further enlarged to take in the Solar System, in all its relations? Nay why may we not go further and suppose them increased to comprehend the Whole created Universe, with all its inhabitants, their various Relations, Dependencies, Duties and necessities. If this is supposable, then a Being of such great Capacity, endowed with sufficient Power, would be an accomplished judge of all rational Beings...would be fit to dispense rewards to Virtue and Punishments to Vice.[23]

Adams' reflections on the nature of otherworldly beings is profound. In another entry, he wrote:

Astronomers tell us, with good reason, that not only all the planets and satellites in our solar system are inhabited, but all the unnumbered worlds that revolve around the fixed stars are inhabited, as well as this globe of Earth. If this is the case, all mankind are no more in comparison of the whole rational creation of God than a point to the orbit of Saturn.[24]

These musings provided rich fodder for discussions between Adams and Washington, who might have explored the moral and theological implications of extraterrestrial life.

Adams' earlier writings questioned whether these beings, if they existed, had sinned and required divine redemption.

"Perhaps all these different ranks of rational beings have in a greater or less degree committed moral wickedness," he speculated. "If so, I ask a Calvinist, whether he will subscribe to this alternative: 'Either God Almighty must assume the respective shapes of all these different species

20

and suffer the penalties of their crimes in their stead, or else all these beings must be consigned to everlasting perdition.'"[25]

As Richard Stockton, a friend and fellow signer of the Declaration of Independence, labeled John Adams "The Atlas of American Independence," it's clear that Adams' intellectual weight was recognized among his peers.[26] Following a compelling speech he delivered in support of independence, Thomas Jefferson described Adams as a "colossus," emphasizing the significant impact he had on the revolutionary movement. In one of his speeches, Adams seemingly prophetically stated, "The second day of July, 1776, will be the most memorable epoch in the history of America...celebrated by succeeding generations as the great anniversary festival." His vision captured the spirit of the nation's founding, tying it to a divine purpose. Indeed, Adam was a deep thinker.[27]

Washington, pragmatic and deeply grounded in the immediate concerns of nation-building, might have approached otherworldly contemplations from a different angle. He would likely have considered the practical implications of discovering extraterrestrial life. How would such a revelation impact the fledgling nation? What measures should be taken to ensure the country's security in the face of unknown cosmic entities?

Both men held a reverence for the divine and the order of the universe.[28] The philosophical and theological dimensions of their discussions would have been enriched by their shared experiences and leadership. In addition, both men understood the significance of unity, knowledge, and preparedness. Adams' diary entries reveal a man who marveled at the vastness of the universe and the potential for other forms of life, while Washington's leadership was characterized by a commitment to reason and the common good.

Adams might have raised the question posed in his diary:

If we examine critically the little Prospect that lies around us at one view[,] we behold an almost infinite Variety of substances.... Now let us for a minute Consider how many million such Prospects there are upon this single Planet, all of which

21

contain as great and some a much Greater Variety of animals and Vegetables. When we have been sufficiently astonished at this incomprehensible multitude of substances, let us rise in our Thoughts and consider, how many Planets and Satellites and Comets there are in this one solar system, each of which has as many such Prospects upon its surface as our Earth.[29]

Washington, a man of practical concerns and deeply rooted in the realities of his time, would have found Adams' speculations a bit disturbing. Washington could have pondered the practical implications: "How would our fledgling nation react to the discovery of beings from other planets? How would we ensure the safety and sovereignty of our people in such an unimaginable scenario?"

Adams, drawing from his philosophical musings, might have replied, "We must prepare our minds and hearts for all possibilities. The universe is vast, and the creation of God is boundless. As we govern and build this nation, we must also look to the stars and consider our place within the grand design of the cosmos."

These potential discussions between Washington and Adams, though speculative, provide an accurate snapshot of the ideas our Founding Fathers explored. Benjamin Franklin, who preceded David Rittenhouse as president of the American Philosophical Society, also speculated about the inhabitants of other worlds as Adam's did in his diary. In his 1728 *Articles of Belief and Acts of Religion*, Franklin wrote:

> For I believe that Man is not the most perfect Being but One, rather that as there are many Degrees of Beings his Inferiors, so there are many Degrees of Beings superior to him.... I CONCEIVE then, that the INFINITE has created many Beings or Gods, vastly superior to Man.... I conceive that each of these is exceeding wise, and good, and very powerful; and that Each has made for himself, one glorious Sun, attended with a beautiful and admirable System of Planets.[30]

Franklin later wrote to Ezra Stiles, president of Yale College, "that the most acceptable Service we can render to him [God], is doing Good to his other Children." Given the context of Franklin's other writings, it is reasonable to conclude that these "other Children" include intelligent beings throughout the universe.

Not everyone from early America saw the inhabitants of other worlds as a good thing. Thomas Paine made a forceful argument against Christianity if extraterrestrial life exists. In his *Age of Reason* (1793), Paine wrote:

> Though it is not a direct article of the Christian system that this world that we inhabit is the whole of the habitable creation, yet it is so worked up therewith from what is called the Mosaic account of the Creation, the story of Eve and the apple, and the counterpart of that story, the death of the Son of God, that to believe otherwise—that is, to believe that God created a plurality of worlds, at least as numerous as what we call stars—renders the Christian system of faith at once little and ridiculous and scatters it in the mind like feathers in the air. The two beliefs cannot be held together in the same mind, and he who thinks that he believes both has thought but little of either.[31]

As we've uncovered in this chapter, America's first two presidents, Washington and Adams, were well aware of the subject of extraterrestrial intelligence. During their eight years of shared administration and the additional four years of Adams' presidency after Washington retired, the presidential office became a place for reflecting on the cosmic musings of men such as David Rittenhouse, Benjamin Franklin, and Thomas Paine. Little did they know that this was the beginning of the White House itself becoming a focal point for discussions and revelations about the mysteries of the universe, including the enduring enigma of unidentified flying objects (UFOs).

The Vision of George Washington

John Adams, a thinker deeply engaged with the vastness of the cosmos, had written extensively on such matters in his youth. His diary entries revealed a mind captivated by the possibilities of an infinite universe filled with rational beings. Due to the renown of his intellect and the caliber of his writing among his fellow revolutionaries, Adams was selected as one of five individuals to draft the Declaration of Independence, joining Thomas Jefferson, Benjamin Franklin, Roger Sherman, and Robert R. Livingston in this important task.

In addition to his philosophical contributions, Adams played a crucial role in the practicalities of the Revolution. When the Second Continental Congress met on May 10, 1775, Adams was appointed chairman of the Board of War and Ordnance, the committee tasked with overseeing the Revolutionary War efforts. As Congress authorized the creation of the Continental Army, Adams put forward George Washington as its commanding general, a decision that would prove to be pivotal for the independence movement.[32] The rest is history.

While these philosophical and scientific discussions grounded in rational inquiry shaped the era, they coexisted with captivating legends that mirrored these cosmic contemplations. One such *legend* is the tale of Washington's vision at Valley Forge. Though *not* considered to be historically genuine, the following tale has captivated imaginations since the Civil War, animating the Founding Fathers' grave contemplation of otherworldly beings.

Amid the freezing winter of 1777–78 at Valley Forge, General George Washington faced not only the harsh elements but the daunting challenge of keeping the Continental Army intact. Desperate for guidance, he often sought solace and strength through prayer. One particularly frigid evening, Washington ventured alone into the snow-covered woods, seeking divine intervention for his beleaguered troops.

As the story goes, Washington knelt in the snow, his breath visible in the icy air, and prayed with fervent intensity. The weight of his responsibilities pressed heavily upon him, and he pleaded for guidance and support in the face of seemingly insurmountable odds. As Washington prayed, the surrounding forest grew eerily quiet. The wind seemed to still, and the usual nocturnal sounds of the woods faded into a profound silence. It was then that Washington sensed a presence unlike any he had felt before. Opening his eyes, he was startled to see a radiant figure standing before him, emanating an otherworldly glow.

The being was neither entirely human nor entirely divine, and its appearance defied earthly description. It spoke to Washington in a voice that resonated with power and serenity, delivering a message of hope and reassurance. The vision imparted knowledge of America's future struggles and triumphs, revealing that the fledgling nation would endure great trials but would ultimately emerge victorious and united.

"Son of the Republic," the being intoned, "look and learn." Washington was shown vivid scenes of future battles and the unfolding destiny of the United States. He saw his army overcoming the British forces, the birth of a new nation, and the enduring spirit of freedom and democracy that would define America.

Washington became inextricably linked to this legend, which has captivated imaginations for generations. Experts believe that the story of "Washington's Vision" originated in the nineteenth century. The account first appeared in print in the 1860s, attributed to an anonymous source who claimed to have heard it from Anthony Sherman, a supposed Revolutionary War veteran. Historians generally regard the tale as apocryphal, recognizing it more as a piece of inspirational folklore than as a historical event.

Though not a piece of verified history, the legend captures the imagination of the Founding Fathers, who pondered the inhabitants of other worlds as a real possibility. This extraordinary vision, whether myth or reality, highlights the profound spiritual and existential questions that preoccupied the thoughts of many of the Founding Fathers. It underscores their contemplation of higher powers and the possibility of otherworldly influences contacting humans. It also reflects a consistent pattern of presidents being at the epicenter of high strangeness, a theme that will be explored in depth throughout this book.

Looking Ahead

As we venture deeper into the enigmatic world of UFO phenomena, our journey from the nascent whispers under Washington and Adams sets the stage for explosive revelations. The skies, once silent and serene, are now filled with mysteries waiting to be unraveled. As Thomas Jefferson assumed the presidency, strange reports of luminous flying objects began to surface, challenging even the sharpest minds of his time. What role did these celestial anomalies play in shaping the early republic's history? The next chapter delves into the extraordinary incidents that reached the desk of the "Declaration President" and explores the unsettling questions they raised about the nature of the universe and our place within it.

Chapter 3

THE DECLARATION PRESIDENT AND
THE REPORTS OF LUMINOUS FLYING OBJECTS

> History, by apprising us of the past, enables us to judge the
> future.
>
> —THOMAS JEFFERSON

As Thomas Jefferson ascended to the presidency in 1801, the weight of both worldly and otherworldly matters began to press heavily upon him. His vice presidency under John Adams had been marked by political strife, philosophical divergence, and the painful dissolution of their once-close friendship. Yet, even in the midst of this political turbulence, there was a shared fascination with the unknown—cosmic mysteries that stretched far beyond the boundaries of the new republic they were building.

Born in 1743 in the rolling hills of Albemarle County, Virginia, Jefferson's early years were shaped by a deep intellectual curiosity. From a young age, he displayed a relentless pursuit of knowledge. As a student, his time was rigorously structured—spending fifteen hours each day poring over his books and three hours practicing the violin, leaving only six hours for eating and sleeping.[33] This disciplined routine not only sharpened his intellect, but also laid the foundation for his future as one of the nation's foremost thinkers and leaders. His intelligence was honed at the College of William and Mary, and it was this keen sense of inquiry that propelled him to the forefront of the American Enlightenment. In 1779, Jefferson became the governor of Virginia, where he faced the challenges of the Revolutionary War, including a sudden British invasion that tested both his leadership and resolve.

Thomas Jefferson suffered the devastating loss of his wife, Martha Wayles Skelton Jefferson, on September 6, 1782, who died after a prolonged illness, likely due to complications from childbirth. Following that personal tragedy, Jefferson reluctantly returned to public life. By 1784, he was appointed to replace Benjamin Franklin as the minister to France, where he spent five years navigating the complexities of French politics and representing the fledgling United States.[34] In 1789, Jefferson returned to America and took up the position of secretary of state under President George Washington, positioning him at the very heart of the new nation's diplomacy and governmental structure.

Yet, it was during his tenure in the Executive Mansion that a singular mystery crossed his desk—one that even his formidable mind could not easily explain.

It was the night of January 16, 1801—just forty-seven days before Jefferson would assume the presidency—while still serving as vice president under John Adams, when he stood before the gathered members of the American Philosophical Society. As president of this esteemed body of thinkers, Jefferson had often led discussions on scientific phenomena and philosophical questions. But this night was different. In his hand, he held a letter from William Dunbar, describing an event that defied reason.

The room grew still as Jefferson prepared to read aloud.

"A phenomenon," he began, his voice steady but laced with curiosity, "was seen to pass Baton Rouge on the night of the 5th of April, 1800."[35] He paused, the weight of the words lingering in the air. "It was first seen in the South West, moving so rapidly over the heads of the spectators that it disappeared in the North East in about a quarter of a minute."[36]

As Jefferson continued to read, the atmosphere in the hall shifted. The men of the Philosophical Society were no strangers to cosmic speculation. David Rittenhouse, the great astronomer, had once mapped the movements of the heavens. Benjamin Franklin had mused about the inhabitants of other worlds. And, as early as 1786, members of the society had recorded observations of meteors and shooting stars, with detailed letters describing such phenomena and read to the society by David Rittenhouse himself.[37] The society had long been a place where the mysteries of the heavens were studied, debated, and categorized. But this—this was different. This was not thought to be a mere comet or meteor.

"It appeared to be of the size of a large house, 70 or 80 feet long," Jefferson continued, "wholly luminous, but not emitting sparks; of a color resembling the sun near the horizon in a cold, frosty evening…a crimson red."[38]

The tension in the chamber in the room thickened as Jefferson's words painted a picture of something extraordinary, otherworldly. The phenomenon described by Jefferson was no ordinary shooting star or comet. It was vast, crimson, and left in its wake a heat so intense that it scorched the forest beneath it.

Jefferson's voice lowered as he recounted the next part of the letter: "A tremendous crash was heard, similar to the largest piece of ordnance, causing a very sensible earthquake."[39]

This object had caused the ground itself to tremble—a tremor that Dunbar compared to the discharge of the heaviest artillery. It had not merely passed through the heavens; it had impacted the earth with violent force.

Jefferson continued, reading with precision: "I have been informed, that search has been made in the place where the burning body fell, and that a considerable portion of the surface of the earth was found broken up, and every vegetable body burned or greatly scorched."[40]

As Jefferson read this part, the mood of those in the parlor grew tense. The object had left a physical mark—scorched earth, broken ground. This wasn't merely an abstract, fleeting event in the sky; it had touched the earth, and its presence had devastated the land beneath it. The men in the room, bound by their belief in the power of reason, now found themselves confronting something that defied the neat categories of their scientific world.

"I have not yet received answers to a number of queries I have sent on," Jefferson added from Dunbar's account, "which may perhaps bring to light more particulars."[41]

At that, the tone of the room shifted again, as if the unanswered questions lingered in the air, waiting to be grasped. The queries Dunbar had sent were likely meant to clarify, to provide rational answers for what had been witnessed. But the delay in response only added to the mystery. Was there more to this event? Could there be details that might further unravel their understanding of the natural world?

Then came a peculiar reference, one that added to the mystery: Figure 5, Plate IV.

"It appeared to be of the size of a large house, 70 or 80 feet long, and of a form nearly resembling **Figure 5 in Plate IV**" (emphasis in original).

At the time, Figure 5 and Plate IV were tangible pieces of evidence seen by the society members. But today, those records are lost to history. What did they reveal? What form did this object take that would require such a detailed illustration? The absence of these crucial pieces only deepens the mystery. Was their loss a simple matter of historical misfortune, or did someone deliberately ensure that these drawings would never see the light of day? Without them, the phenomenon remains a tantalizing enigma, its shape left to the imagination, forever obscured by time.

The Baton Rouge incident, as detailed by Dunbar, described the object as being around two hundred yards above the earth, passing directly over the heads of the spectators. The sheer proximity of such a luminous, enormous body was as shocking as the details that followed. This was no ordinary celestial event. It felt almost as if the heavens themselves had lowered to meet the earth in a cataclysmic display of raw power.

As Jefferson's reading concluded, the weight of the unknown pressed heavily on the gathered scholars. These were men who sought to explain the world through science, through observation and experiment, but the Baton Rouge phenomenon challenged those ideals. It was not a comet or meteor that passed harmlessly through the heavens. It was something else—something larger, more mysterious, and disturbingly real. It had shaken the earth beneath their feet, scorched the land, and disappeared into the night, leaving destruction in its wake.

Twelve years later, after serving as president of the United States from 1801 to 1809, Jefferson received another piece of mail detailing a strange event. In the summer of 1813, a letter arrived from Portsmouth, Virginia, written by Edward Hansford and John Clarke. The account described a phenomenon even more perplexing than the Baton Rouge incident. It wasn't just a fireball streaking across the sky; it was something far more sinister, something…transformative.

"We saw in the South," the letter began, "a ball of fire full as large as the sun at meridian, which was frequently obscured by smoke emitted from its own body."[42] The men described how the object, once resembling a turtle, had risen and fallen, ascending back into the sky before transforming into the shape of a human skeleton. "It then assumed the form of a Scottish Highlander, arrayed for battle, and ultimately passed into the West, disappearing in its own smoke."

This was no ordinary sighting. In a nation still grappling with the Enlightenment's promise of reason and the mysteries of faith, such events rattled the foundations of Jefferson's world. To our knowledge, unlike the Baton Rouge incident, Jefferson did not bring the Portsmouth sighting before the Philosophical Society or his presidential cabinet. Perhaps he felt it too fantastical, too dangerous to the delicate balance of reason the society had so carefully constructed. Or perhaps, like the men who witnessed it, he was beginning to suspect there were forces at play that couldn't easily be explained.

As Jefferson's presidency wore on, these cosmic mysteries hung in the background. The Louisiana Purchase, the Embargo Act, and the young republic's fragile position in a world of empires consumed his days. Yet, as he retired to Monticello, Jefferson could not shake the feeling that there was more—more to the universe than he had once believed.

In his later years, Jefferson reconnected with John Adams, his old friend turned political rival. Their letters, exchanged from 1812 until their deaths, touched on everything from the mechanics of government to the mysteries of the cosmos.[43] Adams, too, had pondered the possibility of life beyond Earth, recording his thoughts in his diary during long, sleepless nights. Their correspondence, including 158 letters in all, was a reflection of two men who had shaped the world, yet remained haunted by the unknown.[44]

On July 4, 1826, exactly fifty years after the Declaration of Independence was signed, both Jefferson and Adams passed away—an eerie symmetry to lives so intertwined with the birth of a nation. Adams' last words, "Thomas Jefferson still lives," echoed the bond they had shared.[45] Yet, unknown to him, Jefferson had already passed, leaving behind a legacy of liberty, reason, and unanswered questions about the mysteries that had once lit up the skies.

Looking Ahead

Years after Jefferson's passing, the skies would again stir with strange phenomena—events that seemed to echo the cosmic mysteries of his time. Between 1896 and 1897, a wave of mysterious "airship" sightings swept across the United States, captivating the public and rekindling the same sense of wonder and confusion that had mystified Jefferson during his presidency.

Though separated by decades, these airship sightings mirrored the unexplained events Jefferson had wrestled with in Baton Rouge and Portsmouth. Were they signs of a technology beyond man's grasp? Or, as the Founders once speculated, were they evidence of forces that defied human understanding?

As the twentieth century approached, the sky's mysteries would only deepen. What had once been the intrigue of America's first presidents would soon evolve into a national concern for leaders across the globe. Roosevelt, Truman, and the presidents who followed would face these phenomena not as fleeting curiosities but as persistent, puzzling, and potentially dangerous forces.

Chapter 4

THE SAUCER PRESIDENTS:
SIGHTINGS, CRASH RETRIEVALS,
THE BIRTH OF THE PHENOMENON

> Objects of the most stupendous magnitude, and measure
> in which the lives and liberties of millions yet unborn are
> intimately interested, are now before us. We are in the very
> midst of a revolution the most complete, unexpected and
> remarkable of any in the history of nations.
>
> —JOHN ADAMS

The Roosevelt Years and Celestial Devices

From the dawn of the American republic under Washington, Adams, and Jefferson, where whispers of otherworldly intrigue began to flicker, we now leap forward to the transformative era of Franklin D. Roosevelt. As Roosevelt guided the nation through the dual crises of the Great Depression and World War II, an enigmatic new challenge began to surface, one that quietly but profoundly altered the course of history: the UFO phenomenon.

On the eve of Halloween in 1938, the CBS radio network aired Orson Welles' dramatic adaptation of *The War of the Worlds*. Despite explicit announcements that the program was a fictional play, its realistic portrayal caused widespread panic among listeners who believed Earth was under alien attack. This incident unearthed a latent fear of extraterrestrial invasion within the American psyche, a fear that would soon be rekindled by real events.

One of the earliest significant UFO-related occurrences during Roosevelt's tenure was an alleged crash near Cape Girardeau, Missouri, in 1941. According to Charlotte Mann, her grandfather, a Baptist minister named William Huffman, was called to the scene of what was presumed to be a plane crash. Instead, Huffman reportedly discovered a circular craft and three deceased humanoid beings. This account, veiled in secrecy and passed down through whispers over generations, suggests an awareness of extraterrestrial visitors long before the famed Roswell, New Mexico, incident.

Not long after the Cape Girardeau event, another mysterious encounter shook the nation. In the night hours of February 25, 1942, air raid sirens sounded throughout Los Angeles, and the city was plunged into a blackout as the military responded to what was believed to be an enemy air attack. Searchlights scanned the skies, and anti-aircraft artillery fired more than 1,400 shells at unidentified objects. Witnesses reported seeing strange lights and objects moving in the sky, some describing them as slow-moving and others as evasive.

The event, which lasted several hours, left the city in a state of high tension. Despite the intense barrage, no enemy aircraft were found, and there was no evidence of a Japanese attack, as initially feared. The military later attributed the incident to a false alarm caused by war nerves and weather balloons, but many witnesses and researchers remain skeptical of this explanation.

Two days later, a leaked memo from President Roosevelt to General George C. Marshall, dated February 27, 1942, referenced recovered "celestial devices" and underscored their potential significance for

national security and technological advancement. The full memo from
Roosevelt read:

> I have considered the disposition of the material in possession
> of the Army that may be of great significance toward the devel-
> opment of a super weapon of war. I disagree with the argument
> that such information should be shared with our ally the Soviet
> Union. Consultation with Dr. Bush and other scientists on the
> issue of finding practical uses for the atomic secrets learned from
> the study of celestial devices precludes any further discussion
> and I therefore authorize Dr. Bush to proceed with the project
> without further delay. The information is vital to the nation's
> superiority and must remain within the confines of state secrets.
> Any further discussion on the matter will be restricted to General
> Donavan, Dr. Bush, the secretary of war, and yourself. The chal-
> lenge our nation faces is daunting and perilous in this undertaking
> and I have committed the resources of the government towards
> that end. You have my assurance that when circumstances are
> favorable and we are victorious, the Army will have the fruits of
> research in exploring further applications of this new wonder.[46]

G. C. Marshall responded to President Roosevelt a week later on
March 5, 1942, and referenced the Los Angeles air raid and the mystery
airplanes that were not *earthly*. This memo said:

> Regarding the air raid over Los Angeles it was learned by Army
> G2 that Rear Admiral Anderson has informed the War Depart-
> ment of a naval recovery of an unidentified airplane off the coast
> of California with no bearing on conventional explanation.
> Further it has been revealed that the Army Air Corps has also
> recovered a similar craft in the San Bernardino Mountains east
> of Los Angeles which cannot be identified as conventional air-
> craft. This Headquarters has come to the determination that the

mystery airplanes are in fact not earthly and according to secret intelligence sources they are in all probability of interplanetary origin. As a consequence I have issued orders to Army G2 that a special intelligence unit be created to further investigate the phenomenon and report any significant connection between recent incidents and those collected by the director of the office of Coordinator of Information.[47]

If these exchanges between Marshall and Roosevelt are genuine, as the available evidence suggests, they represent the first instance in which a US president indicated significant governmental involvement with the UFO phenomenon.

Building upon the clandestine foundation of the Roosevelt administration's interest in advanced technologies, yet another Franklin D. Roosevelt memo is revealing. The memorandum for the Special Committee on Non-Terrestrial Science and Technology, dated February 22, 1944, offers a fascinating glimpse into the strategic considerations of the time. Classified as "DOUBLE TOP SECRET," the memo explicitly acknowledges the possibility of intelligent life beyond Earth—an idea that resonated with earlier American thinkers like John Adams and Benjamin Franklin. In this memo, Roosevelt responds to a proposal from Dr. Vannevar Bush and Professor Albert Einstein to initiate a separate program dedicated to exploring non-terrestrial science, particularly its applications in atomic energy and superweapons. However, Roosevelt opts to defer this initiative, citing the significant costs already incurred by the atomic bomb program and the need to focus on winning the war as quickly as possible. He suggests that this exploratory research should be pursued after the war when resources might be more available. Despite this deferment, Roosevelt expresses a forward-thinking perspective, recognizing the potential benefits of understanding non-terrestrial science for the nation's future security and technological progress. His cautious approach underscores the sensitive nature of this knowledge, particularly regarding its implications for the ongoing atomic bomb project. The memo reads:

I agree with the OSRD proposal of the recommendation put forward by Dr. Bush and Professor Einstein that a separate program be initiated at the earliest possible time. I also agree that application of non-terrestrial know how in atomic energy must be used in perfecting super weapons of war to affect the complete defeat of Germany and Japan. In view of the cost already incurred in the atomic bomb program, it would, at this time, be difficult to approve without further support of the Treasury Department and the military. I therefore have decided to forego such an enterprise. From the point of view of the informed members of the United States, our principle object is not to engage in exploratory research of this kind but to win the war as soon as possible.

Various points have been raised about the difficulties such an endeavor would pose to the already hardened research for advanced weapons programs and support groups in our war effort and I agree that now is not the time. It is my personal judgment that, when the war is won, and peace is once again restored, there will come a time when surplus funds may be available to pursue a program devoted to understanding non-terrestrial science and its technology which is still greatly undiscovered. I have had private discussions with Dr. Bush on this subject and the advice of several eminent scientists who believe the United States should take every advantage of such wonders that have come to us. I have heard the arguments of General Marshall and other members of the military that the United States must assume its destiny in this matter for the sake of the Nation's security in the post-war world and I have given assurances that such will be the case.

I appreciate the effort and time spent in producing valuable insights into the proposal to find ways of advancing our technology and national progress and in coming to grips with the reality that our planet is not the only one harboring intelligent life in the universe. I also commend the committee for the organization and planning that is evident in Dr. Bush's proposal and the delicate way in which it was presented. I trust the committee will appreciate the situation on which this office must render its decision.[48]

The classification "DOUBLE TOP SECRET" adds to the intrigue surrounding this document, indicating the highest level of confidentiality. Although the authenticity of this memo is subject to debate, it remains a fascinating piece of historical lore that suggests a high-level governmental acknowledgment of extraterrestrial phenomena during Roosevelt's presidency.

The Truman Years and the UFOs Over the White House

When Harry Truman assumed the presidency in 1945, he inherited a world in transition from the devastation of World War II to the escalating tensions of the Cold War. Amidst these global challenges, Truman also confronted the perplexing reality of unexplained aerial phenomena, testing his leadership in unprecedented ways.

The term "flying saucer" became part of the public lexicon following Kenneth Arnold's notable sighting near Mount Rainier in 1947. Arnold, an aviator, businessman, and politician, reported seeing nine crescent-shaped objects moving at extraordinary speeds, which he likened to saucers skipping across water. This sighting, widely publicized and sensationalized, marked the advent of the modern era of UFO encounters.

The most renowned incident of 1947, however, was the Roswell, New Mexico, crash. In July 1947, a rancher named Mac Brazel discovered strange debris on his property near Roswell. The debris included metallic fragments, rubber strips, and other unusual materials. Brazel reported his find to the local sheriff, who contacted the nearby Roswell Army Air Field. Major Jesse Marcel, an intelligence officer, was sent to investigate and collect the debris.

On July 8, 1947, the Roswell Army Air Field issued a press release stating they had recovered a "flying disc." However, this statement was quickly retracted, and a subsequent press release claimed the debris was from a weather balloon. Despite the official explanation, many witnesses, including Marcel, later stated the debris was unlike anything they had ever seen and suggested a cover-up.

The Roswell incident remained relatively obscure until the late 1970s when researchers and witnesses began to come forward with new information. Claims of alien bodies being recovered and a government cover-up fueled public interest and speculation. The Roswell incident has since become the most famous UFO case in history, inspiring countless books, documentaries, and conspiracy theories.

Adding to the intrigue, a month before Roswell, harbor patrolman Harold Dahl reported of doughnut-shaped objects over Puget Sound, one of which exploded, showering his boat with debris. The subsequent deaths of two Army Air Force officers investigating the case deepened the mystery. Although Dahl later retracted his story, many believe he was coerced into silence. (For more details about this incident, see page 43.)

Truman's administration also grappled with the 1952 Washington DC UFO incident. As Larry Holcombe chronicles in his book, *The Presidents and UFOs*, on the weekends of July 19–20 and July 26–27, 1952, unidentified flying objects were detected in the restricted airspace over the US Capitol and the White House. These objects were tracked on radar at both Washington National Airport and Andrews Air Force Base. The first incident began late on July 19, around 11:40 p.m., and continued until 5:30 the next morning, while the sightings on July 26 started at 8:15 p.m. and lasted until dawn.[49]

Air Force and Pentagon spokesperson Albert Chop was alerted to these events, leading to the deployment of Air Force jets on the night of July 19. However, the mysterious objects evaded interception, disappearing when the jets approached and reappearing once they returned to base. During the incidents on July 26, these objects displayed extraordinary behavior, accelerating at speeds estimated to exceed seven thousand miles per hour and demonstrating flight characteristics that puzzled military personnel. The events were witnessed by thousands, including civilians and military personnel, and were extensively documented through photographs and global news coverage.

As public anxiety escalated, President Truman directed General Robert B. Landry to contact the Pentagon on July 27 for detailed information, concerned that the situation could spiral out of control. In response, Air Force Generals John Samford and Roger Ramey held a press conference on July 29—the most significant since World War II—to alleviate public concerns. They attributed the sightings to misidentified stars and radar anomalies caused by temperature inversions. While this explanation was largely accepted by the public, it was met with skepticism within the military. Radar operators felt their credibility was being questioned, and atmospheric physicist Dr. James E. McDonald dismissed the explanation as scientifically implausible. Even Capt. Edward J. Ruppelt, the head of Project Blue Book, later expressed reservations about the official narrative in his writings[50]

UFO Sightings and Crash Retrievals

As we transition from the tumultuous years of Roosevelt and Truman, marked by unprecedented governmental encounters with the unknown, our journey into the mysterious skies continues. From the secretive incidents during World War II to the escalating Cold War fears surrounding flying saucers, it becomes clear that humanity's experiences with unexplained aerial phenomena stretch back for centuries. To truly grasp the depth and breadth of these phenomena, we must explore some of the most notorious and well-documented sightings and crash retrievals—moments when the mysteries of the skies first began to captivate and terrify.

1947: Kenneth Arnold Sighting, USA

On June 24, 1947, private pilot Kenneth Arnold was flying near Mount Rainier, Washington, when he observed nine unusual objects flying in formation. Arnold described them as being crescent-shaped and moving at incredible speeds. He estimated their speed to be more than 1,200 miles per hour, far beyond the capabilities of any known aircraft at the time.

Arnold's sighting received widespread media attention, and he described the objects as moving "like a saucer would if you skipped it across the water." This led to the coining of the term "flying saucer," which became a popular way to refer to UFOs. What Arnold saw is often considered the beginning of the modern UFO era, sparking a wave of similar reports across the United States and around the world.

Despite extensive investigations, Arnold's sighting remains unexplained. Some researchers have suggested he might have seen a formation of secret military aircraft or an optical illusion, but no definitive explanation has been provided. Arnold's credibility and detailed account make his sighting one of the most significant and influential in UFO history.

1947: Maury Island Incident, USA

On June 21, 1947, in the incident briefly mentioned earlier, Harold Dahl, a harbor patrolman, reported seeing six doughnut-shaped objects near Maury Island in Washington State. According to Dahl, one of the objects exploded, showering his boat with metallic debris and injuring his son and dog. Dahl contacted his supervisor, Fred Crisman, who also claimed to have seen the objects and collected samples of the debris.

The incident attracted the attention of military intelligence, and two Army Air Force officers, Captain William Davidson and Lieutenant Frank Brown, were dispatched to investigate. After interviewing Dahl and Crisman and collecting some of the debris, the officers died in a plane crash while transporting the materials. The official explanation was that the crash was an accident, but many speculated that it was related to the UFO investigation.

Dahl later retracted his story, stating it was a hoax, but many believe he was coerced into doing so. The Maury Island incident remains controversial, with some researchers arguing it was a precursor to the modern UFO era. The involvement of military intelligence and the mysterious deaths of Davidson and Brown have kept the incident alive in UFO lore.

1954: Florence, Italy

On October 27, 1954, during a football match in Florence, thousands of spectators at the *Stadio Artemio Franchi* witnessed multiple UFOs hovering above the stadium. The objects were described as luminous, cigar-shaped, and disc-like, moving silently and at high speeds. The match was temporarily halted as players and fans alike watched the objects in awe.

One of the most notable aspects of the Florence sighting was the fall of a strange, silvery substance from the sky, later dubbed "angel hair." This material reportedly disintegrated upon contact, leaving no trace. Witnesses included many reliable individuals, such as the referee, players, and journalists covering the match, all of whom provided consistent accounts of the event.

The Florence UFO sighting remains one of the most remarkable mass sightings in Europe, both for the number of witnesses and the mysterious angel-hair phenomenon. Despite various theories, including spiders' webs and atmospheric conditions, the true nature of the sighting and the substance remains unexplained.

1955: Levelland, Texas, USA

On the night of November 2, 1957, multiple residents of Levelland, Texas, reported seeing glowing objects that affected their car engines and electronics. Witnesses described the objects as bright, oval-shaped, and emitting a blue-green light. As the objects approached, car engines would stall and lights would dim, only to return to normal once the objects moved away.

Police officers and numerous civilians provided consistent reports of the phenomenon, leading to an extensive investigation by the Air Force. Project Blue Book, the Air Force's UFO investigation program, concluded that the sightings were caused by an electrical storm and ball lightning, though many witnesses disagreed with this explanation.

The Levelland sightings are significant for the large number of independent witnesses and the physical effects reported. The incident remains among the most compelling UFO cases involving interactions with vehicles and continues to be a subject of interest for UFO researchers.

1965: Exeter Incident, USA

On September 3, 1965, Norman Muscarello, an eighteen-year-old resident of Exeter, New Hampshire, reported seeing a large, bright object with pulsating lights near a farm. Muscarello flagged down a police car, and Officer Eugene Bertrand accompanied him back to the site. They observed the object hovering silently, emitting red and white lights and moving in a manner that defied conventional aircraft capabilities.

Officer David Hunt, who also responded to the report, corroborated the sighting. The object eventually ascended and disappeared into the sky. The incident drew significant media attention, and Project Blue Book investigated the case, concluding that the witnesses had observed a weather balloon or a misidentified aircraft, though many remain skeptical of this explanation.

The Exeter incident is notable for the involvement of multiple police officers and the consistency of their testimonies. The sighting remains unexplained and is considered another of the most credible and well-documented UFO encounters of the 1960s.

1966: Westall, Australia

On April 6, 1966, more than two hundred students and teachers at Westall High School in Melbourne, Australia, witnessed an extraordinary event. Around 11 a.m., a silver, saucer-shaped craft was seen descending into a nearby grassy field known as the Grange. Witnesses described the object as being about the size of two cars, metallic in appearance, and producing a faint humming noise. The craft hovered for a few minutes, landed briefly, then took off at a high speed.

The sighting caused a frenzy among the students and staff, many of whom ran towards the field to get a closer look. Some reported seeing two smaller aircraft nearby that seemed to be observing or accompanying the larger object. Teachers attempted to maintain order, but the event left a lasting impression on those who witnessed it. Despite numerous eyewitness accounts, the Australian government and military provided no official explanation.

The Westall UFO incident remains one of Australia's most well-documented and compelling UFO cases. The large number of credible witnesses, the detailed descriptions, and the lack of an official explanation have made it a cornerstone event in UFO research. It continues to be a subject of fascination and debate among researchers and the general public.

1967: Shag Harbour Incident, Canada

On the night of October 4, 1967, residents of Shag Harbour, a small fishing village in Nova Scotia, witnessed a series of strange lights in the sky. Multiple witnesses, including Royal Canadian Mounted Police (RCMP) officers, observed a large, illuminated object crash into the waters of Shag Harbour. The object was described as a series of flashing orange lights that moved in formation before descending rapidly into the harbor.

Local fishermen and the RCMP quickly responded, expecting to find a downed aircraft. They searched the waters but found no debris or survivors. Divers from the Royal Canadian Navy conducted an underwater search the following day; again, no evidence of a crash was found. The incident was thoroughly investigated by both civilian and military authorities, neither of whom provided a definitive explanation.

The Shag Harbour incident is notable for the number of solid witnesses, including police officers and military personnel, and the detailed documentation of the event. It remains one of the best-documented UFO cases in Canada and is often cited as yet another of the most credible UFO sightings in the world.

1969: Berwyn Mountain Incident, Wales

On January 23, 1974, residents near Berwyn Mountain in North Wales reported seeing a bright light in the sky, followed by a loud explosion and tremors that shook the area. Many locals believed an aircraft had crashed on the mountainside, and rescue teams were dispatched to search for wreckage and survivors.

Upon arriving at the scene, searchers found no evidence of a crash or debris. Some witnesses reported seeing mysterious lights moving across the mountainside, leading to speculation about a UFO crash. The official explanation attributed the event to a combination of an earthquake and a meteor sighting, but many locals remained unconvinced.

The Berwyn Mountain incident has since become a subject of intense debate and investigation. Some researchers believe a UFO did indeed crash, and the event was covered up by authorities. The lack of concrete evidence and the conflicting reports continue to fuel speculation about and interest in the case.

1973: Coyne Helicopter Incident, USA

On October 18, 1973, a US Army Reserve helicopter crew, led by Captain Lawrence Coyne, experienced a close encounter with a UFO near Mansfield, Ohio. The crew was flying at an altitude of 2,500 feet when they noticed a bright, red light approaching rapidly from the east. The object, described as a cigar-shaped craft with a dome on top, stopped abruptly in front of the helicopter and emitted a green beam of light.

The green beam appeared to lift the helicopter, causing the altimeter to climb rapidly without any input from the pilot. The encounter lasted for several minutes before the UFO ascended and disappeared into the night sky. The crew, which included medical personnel, provided detailed and consistent accounts of the incident. Ground witnesses also reported seeing the UFO and the helicopter.

The Coyne helicopter incident is another one considered to be among the most credible UFO encounters due to the professional background of the witnesses and the detailed documentation of the event. The US Army conducted an investigation, but found no conventional explanation. The case remains a significant example of a military encounter with a UFO.

1976: Tehran UFO Incident, Iran

On the night of September 18, 1976, multiple witnesses in Tehran, Iran, observed a luminous object in the sky. The Iranian Air Force scrambled two F-4 Phantom jets to intercept the object. The first jet experienced instrumentation failure as it approached the UFO, so had to return to base. The second, piloted by Lieutenant Parviz Jafari, continued the pursuit.

Jafari reported that the object produced a bright light that temporarily blinded him and his copilot. The UFO displayed advanced maneuvers, including rapid ascents and descents, and released smaller objects that approached the jet at high speeds. Jafari attempted to fire a missile at the object, but his weapons systems malfunctioned. The UFO eventually sped away at an incredible speed, and the jets returned to base.

The Tehran incident was investigated by the US Defense Intelligence Agency, which documented the event in a detailed report. The case remains unexplained, with the advanced maneuvers and electronic disruptions experienced by the pilots defying conventional explanations. The Tehran UFO encounter is considered one of the most significant military UFO cases in history.

1980: Rendlesham Forest Incident, UK

Between December 26 and 28, 1980, US military personnel stationed at Royal Air Force (RAF) Woodbridge in Suffolk, England, reported a series of UFO sightings and encounters in the nearby Rendlesham Forest. On the first night, security police officers John Burroughs and Jim Penniston observed strange lights descending into the forest. Upon investigation, they encountered a triangular craft with hieroglyphic-like markings. Penniston reportedly touched the craft, which emitted a bright light and left indentations in the ground.

The following nights saw further sightings and investigations, including by Deputy Base Commander Lieutenant Colonel Charles Halt, who recorded his observations on an audiotape. Halt and his team observed multiple lights, including a red object that split into smaller lights and shot beams of light to the ground. The events were documented in Halt's official memo and have been the subject of extensive investigation and debate.

The Rendlesham Forest incident is often referred to as "Britain's Roswell" and remains one of the most well-documented and compelling UFO cases. The credibility of the military witnesses, physical evidence, and detailed accounts have made it a cornerstone of UFO research and a subject of ongoing interest and controversy.

1986: Japan Airlines Flight 1628, USA

On November 17, 1986, Japan Airlines Flight 1628, a cargo flight from Paris to Tokyo, encountered a massive UFO while flying over Alaska. The flight crew, led by Captain Kenju Terauchi, observed two small, fast-moving objects that approached their aircraft. These objects were followed by a large, walnut-shaped craft, which Terauchi estimated to be twice the size of an aircraft carrier.

The UFO was tracked on radar by both the aircraft and ground control, and the crew described the craft as having a bright light that illuminated the cockpit. Despite attempts to guide the plane to evade the craft, it continued to shadow the plane for approximately fifty minutes before disappearing. The encounter was reported to the Federal Aviation Administration (FAA), which conducted a thorough investigation. Captain Terauchi's detailed testimony, along with radar data and corroborating reports from other aircraft in the area, provided substantial evidence of the encounter. Despite this, the FAA's official analysis was inconclusive, leaving the incident unexplained.

The Japan Airlines Flight 1628 sighting is considered yet one more solid UFO case due to the detailed observations by experienced pilots and the involvement of radar data. It has been the subject of numerous documentaries and research papers, highlighting the challenges in explaining such encounters with conventional theories.

1989-1990: Belgium UFO Wave

From November 1989 to April 1990, Belgium experienced a wave of UFO sightings, with thousands of witnesses—including police officers and military personnel—reporting large, triangular objects with bright lights. The objects were described as silent, as capable of hovering and rapid acceleration, and often as having three lights at their vertices and a red light in the center.

One of the most significant encounters occurred on the night of March 30–31, 1990, when the Belgian Air Force scrambled two F-16 fighter jets to intercept the unidentified objects. The jets' radar detected the UFOs, which performed maneuvers that defied conventional aircraft capabilities, including rapid descents and right-angle turns. Despite multiple attempts, the jets were unable to lock onto the objects, which eventually disappeared.

The Belgian UFO wave was extensively documented and investigated by the Belgian Society for the Study of Space Phenomena, which collected hundreds of witness reports and photographs. The involvement of the military and the detailed radar data are why this is on the list of the most credible and well-documented mass UFO sightings. The incidents remain unexplained, contributing to the enduring mystery of the UFO phenomenon.

1997: Phoenix Lights, USA

On the evening of March 13, 1997, thousands of people across Arizona and Nevada in the United States, as well as residents of the Mexican state of Sonora, reported seeing a series of lights in a V-shaped formation moving silently across the sky. The lights were observed over a wide area, including the city of Phoenix, Arizona, where residents described seeing a massive, boomerang-shaped object blocking out the stars.

The event was witnessed by a diverse group of people, including pilots, police officers, and the governor of Arizona, Fife Symington, who later said he saw the lights and confirmed their unusual nature. The lights were also captured on video by multiple witnesses, further adding to the legitimacy of the sighting. The US Air Force later stated the lights were flares dropped by A-10 aircraft during a training exercise, but many witnesses and researchers remain skeptical of this explanation.

The Phoenix Lights incident is one of the most widely reported and well-documented mass UFO sightings in history. The large number of trustworthy witnesses, the extensive media coverage, and the ongoing debate about the true nature of the lights make it a cornerstone event in UFO research.

1999: Narrowsburg, New York, USA

On August 30, 1999, several residents of Narrowsburg, New York, reported seeing a large, triangular UFO with bright lights. The object was described as silent and moving slowly across the sky, with a distinctive triangular shape and bright white lights at each corner. Witnesses included local police officers and residents who provided consistent and detailed descriptions of the craft.

The sighting prompted an investigation by local authorities and UFO researchers, who collected witness testimonies and attempted to identify any conventional explanations. Despite extensive efforts, no aircraft or other conventional sources could be identified that matched the descriptions provided by the witnesses. The incident remains unexplained and has been documented in various UFO publications and reports.

The Narrowsburg sighting is notable for the detailed and consistent witness accounts and the involvement of local law enforcement. It adds to the growing body of evidence supporting the existence of large, triangular UFOs and remains a significant case in the study of unexplained aerial phenomena.

2000: Southern Illinois, USA

In January 2000, multiple police officers in southern Illinois reported sightings of a large, triangular UFO. The sightings began around 4 a.m., when Officer Ed Barton of the Highland Police Department observed a bright, triangular object moving silently in the sky. Barton radioed a description of what he saw to nearby departments, leading to additional reports from officers in Lebanon, Shiloh, and Millstadt.

The officers described the object as having bright white lights at each corner and a red light in the center. The craft was reported to be flying at a low altitude and moving slowly across the sky. Attempts to track the object with radar were unsuccessful, and no conventional aircraft could be identified that matched the accounts provided. The incident received significant media coverage and was investigated by MUFON (Mutual UFO Network).

The Southern Illinois sighting is considered one of the strongest triangular UFO cases due to the involvement of multiple police officers and the detailed documentation of the event. The consistency of the witness reports and the lack of a conventional explanation continue to make it a subject of interest for UFO researchers.

2004: Tinley Park Lights, USA

On August 21, 2004, numerous residents of Tinley Park, Illinois, observed a series of red lights forming a triangular pattern in the sky. The lights moved slowly and silently, remaining visible for an extended period. Witnesses described the lights as bright red and evenly spaced, creating a distinctive triangular formation.

The sighting was captured on video by several residents, and the footage was analyzed by UFO researchers and experts. Despite various theories, including weather balloons and military flares, no definitive explanation was found. The account received extensive media coverage and was investigated by local authorities and UFO organizations.

The Tinley Park lights are significant because of the large number of witnesses, the clear video evidence, and the unexplained nature of the sighting. The incident is often cited as one of the most compelling UFO cases of the early 2000s and continues to be a subject of interest for researchers and enthusiasts.

2006: O'Hare Airport, USA

On November 7, 2006, multiple employees at O'Hare International Airport in Chicago reported seeing a saucer-shaped craft hovering over the terminal. The object was described as a metallic, disc-shaped craft that remained stationary for several minutes before shooting upwards at a high speed, leaving a hole in the cloud cover.

Witnesses included airport workers, pilots, and ground crew, all of whom provided consistent accounts of the sighting. The incident was reported to the FAA, but officials initially denied any knowledge of the event. After media coverage and pressure from witnesses, the FAA acknowledged the reports but attributed the sighting to weather phenomena.

The O'Hare Airport sighting remains one of the most plausible UFO cases involving a major international airport. The large number of reliable witnesses and the physical evidence of the hole in the cloud cover make this a key case in the study of UFO phenomena. Despite the official explanation, many researchers and observers remain convinced the object was an unidentified craft.

2007: Alderney, Channel Islands

On April 23, 2007, Captain Ray Bowyer, a commercial airline pilot for Aurigny Air Services, reported seeing a UFO during a flight from Southampton, England, to Alderney in the Channel Islands. Bowyer described the object as a bright yellow light with a dark center, and larger than an aircraft. He observed it for several minutes as it remained stationary in the sky before disappearing.

Bowyer's sighting was corroborated by passengers on his flight and another pilot flying in the area. Ground radar also detected an unidentified object at the same time. The sighting was investigated by the British Civil Aviation Authority and the Ministry of Defence, but no conventional explanation was provided.

The Alderney incident is significant due to the credibility of the witnesses and the involvement of radar data, making it one of the most reliable UFO sightings involving commercial aircraft. Captain Bowyer's detailed observations and the corroborative evidence provided by other pilots and radar operators contribute to the ongoing interest and research into the case.

2008: Stephenville, Texas, USA

In January 2008, numerous residents of Stephenville, Texas, reported seeing large, silent craft with bright lights. The objects were described as being enormous, some as wide as a mile, and performing high-speed maneuvers. Witnesses included local citizens, police officers, and pilots, all of whom provided consistent accounts of the sightings.

One of the most notable witnesses was Steve Allen, a private pilot and businessman who described seeing a massive craft with bright, pulsating lights. The sightings continued for several weeks, drawing significant media attention and prompting an investigation by MUFON. Radar data obtained through a Freedom of Information Act request showed unidentified objects in the area at the time of the sightings, further corroborating witness reports.

The Stephenville sightings remain unexplained and are considered among the most noteworthy UFO cases of the twenty-first century due to the large number of credible witnesses and the supporting radar evidence. The incident has been featured in numerous documentaries and articles, contributing to the ongoing debate about the existence of unidentified aerial phenomena.

2009: Turkey

Between 2007 and 2009, multiple reports and videos surfaced of UFOs over Istanbul and other parts of Turkey. The most notable of these sightings occurred in the Kumburgaz area, where a security guard named Yalcin Yalman captured several hours of video footage of strange, disc-shaped objects hovering over the Sea of Marmara. The videos, taken with a high-powered camera, showed detailed views of the craft, including what appeared to be occupants inside.

The footage was analyzed by experts and deemed authentic, with no signs of tampering or manipulation. Witnesses in the area reported seeing the objects on multiple occasions, adding credibility to Yalman's recordings. The Turkish National Observatory and other scientific institutions conducted investigations, but were unable to provide a conventional explanation.

The Turkey UFO videos are considered some of the strongest visual evidence of unidentified flying objects. The detailed footage and the consistency of witness reports have made this case a focal point for UFO researchers and enthusiasts worldwide.

Looking Ahead

As we reflect on the UFO encounters and celestial phenomena that began in the Roosevelt and Truman years, it's evident that these moments were more than mere blips on the radar—they became deeply ingrained in the fabric of American history and global consciousness. What started as whispered tales of extraterrestrial visitors in Missouri and flashing lights over Los Angeles evolved into widespread public curiosity and governmental acknowledgment. These early presidential encounters with the unknown laid the foundation for decades of inquiry, secrecy, and speculation that have continued to this day.

The exchange between President Franklin D. Roosevelt and General Marshall reveals that the highest levels of government not only were aware of unidentified phenomena, but they considered them of utmost national security importance. If the memos and classified reports of advanced "celestial devices" are indeed genuine, they represent the dawn of a new era—one in which UFOs are no longer the domain of science fiction, but are a real, pressing matter for military and scientific leaders alike. Harry Truman's presidency, marked by the infamous Roswell crash and UFOs flying over the White House, further solidified the enduring presence of these phenomena in the national psyche.

As the UFO phenomenon progressed into the mid-twentieth century, it became clear that humanity was no longer alone in contemplating
the skies. The military's engagement with unidentified crafts during the
Roosevelt and Truman administrations, paired with increasing public
awareness, cemented these encounters as key historical touchpoints.
The legacy of these "flying saucer presidents" set the stage for future
administrations to grapple with the delicate balance of public curiosity, government secrecy, and the ever-present possibility that we are not
alone in the universe.

But it was President Dwight D. Eisenhower who would soon take
these mysterious encounters to an entirely new level. Whispers of secret
meetings and direct contact with extraterrestrial beings during his
administration began to circulate. Was there truth behind these rumors?
Did the leader who forged alliances in war also forge alliances beyond
this world? Eisenhower's presidency would mark a turning point—
where UFOs shifted from being a series of isolated incidents to a matter
of deep governmental secrecy, possibly shaping policies that remain classified to this day.

The phenomenon that began in the shadows of war would grow into
one of the most enduring and tantalizing mysteries of modern times.
Whether these encounters were glimpses into the future of human discovery or the vestiges of government secrecy, their legacy is one that
continues to intrigue and mystify to this very day. The story of UFOs is
far from over, and as history unfolds, the truth may eventually come to
light. In the next chapter, we will explore how Eisenhower's administration navigated these phenomena, and whether the whispered meetings
with extraterrestrials were more than just rumors.

LIBERTY DOG

Chapter 5

THE ENCOUNTER PRESIDENT
AND "ALIEN" ABDUCTIONS

> The natural progress of things is for liberty to yield, and
> government to gain ground.
>
> —THOMAS JEFFERSON

Eisenhower and the Cosmic Conspiracy

In the cold desert night of February 20, 1954, President Dwight D. Eisenhower, supposedly enjoying a quiet vacation in Palm Springs, vanished without a trace for several hours. The official story—a chipped tooth and an emergency trip to a dentist—barely made headlines. But for those paying attention, something far more extraordinary was at play. Whispers among the well-connected told a different story: Eisenhower wasn't with a dentist that night. Instead, he was at Edwards Air Force Base, locked in a secret meeting with beings from another world.

This isn't just another tale lost to the annals of conspiracy. For decades, a carefully maintained narrative of secrecy, silence, and subtle power plays has surrounded the man who once led the free world and these mysterious visitors from beyond. As we peel back the layers of this extraordinary story, it becomes clear that Eisenhower wasn't just any president. He was the gatekeeper to one of the greatest secrets ever kept from humanity.

The Vanishing Act: Meeting the Visitors

According to multiple accounts, on that fateful night in February 1954, Eisenhower was quietly whisked away from his vacation retreat to Edwards Air Force Base in complete secrecy. Awaiting him on the runway weren't military officers or political allies, but UFOs—two alien spacecraft that had descended from the sky. As the president's plane touched down, one of the crafts hovered protectively overhead, while the other landed smoothly on the tarmac. Eisenhower, in what some claim was an unprecedented move, left his entourage behind and approached the alien craft alone.

The beings that emerged, often described as tall, human-like figures with blond hair—dubbed the "Nordics"—stood before the most powerful man on Earth. What followed was a conversation that would forever alter the course of human history. The visitors reportedly issued a dire ultimatum: Disarm your nuclear weapons, or face devastating consequences.

But Eisenhower, the supreme commander who had led the Allies to victory in World War II, wasn't a man who cowered easily. He knew nuclear disarmament could tip the balance of power in the Cold War, placing the United States in a position of vulnerability. Still, the conversation didn't end in stalemate. A deal—more sinister than anyone could have imagined—was allegedly struck. In exchange for extraterrestrial technology, Eisenhower is believed to have granted permission for the abduction of a limited number of humans, as long as their activities remained covert. It was a chilling compromise, one some believe the president made in the interest of preserving America's security in a volatile world.

Foo Fighters and the Beginnings of a Cosmic Awareness

To understand how a man like Eisenhower could have been thrust into such an otherworldly position, we must trace his connection to the UFO phenomenon back to the days of World War II. As the supreme Allied commander, Eisenhower oversaw operations in Europe and the Pacific, where reports of mysterious "foo fighters" began to surface. Pilots from both the Allied and Axis forces reported seeing strange, glowing orbs following their aircraft. These fast-moving objects defied the laws of physics, darting through the sky with unmatched speed and agility.

Although dismissed at the time as enemy technology or atmospheric anomalies, foo fighters represented the first cracks in the facade of earthly certainty. By the time Eisenhower assumed the presidency in 1953, the sightings of unidentified flying objects had only intensified. These were not isolated incidents, but a worldwide phenomenon that was becoming increasingly impossible to ignore.

One key event that would have landed on Eisenhower's radar was the infamous 1942 Battle of Los Angeles. In the early morning hours of February 25, anti-aircraft guns unleashed a barrage of fire into the sky over Los Angeles in response to what many believed was a UFO. While official reports blamed the chaos on weather balloons or wartime jitters, the incident raised more questions than answers. If the Roosevelt-Marshall memos regarding this event are to be believed, Eisenhower would have been informed of these mysteries as one of General Marshall's most trusted commanders.

The Churchill Connection: A Pact of Silence

Eisenhower's education in the cosmic unknown didn't stop with battlefield reports. Toward the end of World War II, Eisenhower met with British Prime Minister Winston Churchill to discuss an unsettling event—a sighting by an RAF pilot of a UFO hovering near the English coastline. The craft was unlike anything the Allies or the Axis had in their arsenals. Churchill, a pragmatic leader who understood the power of public perception, allegedly turned to Eisenhower and said, "This event must be immediately classified. If it were to become public, it would create mass panic and destroy the faith people have in the church."

From that moment forward, the men who shaped the outcome of the war were bound by a silent understanding: The world was not ready for the truth.

Majestic-12: Eisenhower's Role in the Secret Government

By the time Eisenhower took office, UFO sightings were reaching a fever pitch. The infamous 1952 Washington, DC, incident saw UFOs swarm the skies over the nation's capital, sparking widespread panic. The government could no longer ignore the growing wave of public and military sightings, but the official stance remained one of silence. Behind closed doors, however, a select few were dealing with the issue head on.

Eisenhower inherited the cloak-and-dagger world of Majestic-12 (MJ-12), a secretive group tasked with overseeing the UFO phenomenon and extraterrestrial matters. According to the Eisenhower Briefing Document, leaked in the 1980s, the president was informed of the earlier-mentioned 1947 Roswell incident, wherein a UFO crash allegedly resulted in the recovery of extraterrestrial bodies. MJ-12, originally formed under Truman's administration, had continued into Eisenhower's presidency; its mandate: to control the dissemination of all UFO-related information.

The briefing told Eisenhower what he likely already suspected—that something far greater than Cold War politics was happening. UFOs weren't just sightings in the sky. They represented an entirely new reality, one that demanded the utmost secrecy.

The Holloman Air Force Base Encounter: The Cosmic Summit

The most astounding chapter in Eisenhower's involvement with extraterrestrials came a year after the Edwards Air Force Base incident. In

February 1955, while on a hunting trip in Georgia, Eisenhower allegedly made a secret trip to Holloman Air Force Base in New Mexico. Witnesses claimed that two UFOs appeared over the airstrip that day. One hovered above, while the other landed in front of the president's plane. What happened next, according to multiple sources, was a second meeting between Eisenhower and extraterrestrials.

The details are scarce, but the implications are profound. Eisenhower was no longer merely the president of the United States; he had become the central figure in an interplanetary negotiation. Some believe this meeting solidified the secret agreements made at Edwards—a continuation of the covert pact between humanity and extraterrestrial visitors.

The Farewell Address: A Cryptic Warning

As Eisenhower's presidency drew to a close in 1961, he delivered a farewell address that has become one of the most analyzed speeches in American history. He warned of the growing power of the "military-industrial complex," a coalition of defense contractors and military leaders that was exerting increasing control over the government.

For those who study the UFO phenomenon, this warning was far more than a critique of corporate influence. It was a veiled reference to the shadowy organizations like MJ-12 that had taken control of UFO research and the extraterrestrial narrative.

Eisenhower had seen the balance of power shift away from the hands of elected officials and into the grasp of secretive military-industrial alliances that now held the keys to the UFO mystery. His warning to the American people, though cryptic, was his last attempt to shine light on the growing darkness of hidden agendas.

The Legacy of a Cosmic Guardian

What Eisenhower knew, and how much of it he took to his grave, may never be fully revealed. But the pieces of his legacy are scattered throughout history, waiting to be assembled. From his secret meetings with extraterrestrials to his involvement with Majestic-12, Eisenhower was at the center of a cosmic conspiracy that continues to ripple through the corridors of power.

As Eisenhower played his final rounds of golf and retired to his farm in Gettysburg, did he reflect on the decisions he made? Did he ponder the implications of the deal he brokered, the secrecy he enforced? Did he worry that humanity's future was tied to forces beyond his control? We may never know.

But one thing is clear: Dwight D. Eisenhower wasn't just the president who led America through the Cold War. He was a gatekeeper to a secret far larger than any earthly conflict—one that, one day, may change the course of human history.

And, perhaps, in his final moments, Eisenhower carried the weight of that secret with him—the knowledge that we are not alone, and that the greatest truths are often the ones we're not yet ready to face.

Other Encounters from Beyond: Echoes of the Unknown

If true, Eisenhower's meetings with extraterrestrials set the stage for a hidden agenda that shaped the future of human-alien contact. But the consequences of those secret dealings didn't end with his administration. In fact, the modern era is rife with accounts of alien encounters and abductions that appear to trace back to the moment Eisenhower allegedly brokered a deal with beings from another world.

For decades, unexplained sightings and eerie abductions have captivated the public, sparking whispers that these events might stem from shadowy agreements made in the 1950s, when the US government first grappled with the reality of UFOs. While President Eisenhower's direct involvement remains speculative, the strange events that followed his presidency cast a long and unsettling shadow. Stories of contact with beings from beyond our world persist, stretching the boundaries of belief yet continuing to surface through countless eyewitness accounts.

From the quiet banks of the Pascagoula River to the remote forests of Arizona, from a schoolyard in Zimbabwe to the narrow streets of a Brazilian town, these encounters hint at a reality far larger than we may be able to comprehend. Whether these modern events are directly connected to decisions made in secret decades ago remains uncertain, but the stories themselves show no signs of fading away.

The Pascagoula Abduction: A Night by the River

It was October 11, 1973, and the evening air along the Pascagoula River in Mississippi was warm and still. Charles Hickson and Calvin Parker, two shipyard workers, were hoping for a peaceful night of fishing. Instead, they found themselves at the center of a mystery that would baffle the world.

As they sat along the riverbank, a strange blue light appeared in the sky, reflecting off the dark water. At first, they thought it was just the lights of a police car. But as they turned to investigate, they saw something they could not have imagined: A smooth, glowing craft hovered silently above the river. It was oval, eerily still, and otherworldly. Before they could react, a hissing sound filled the air, and from the craft emerged beings that defied description.

The creatures were unlike anything they had ever seen—grey-skinned, with strange robotic movements, and pincers for hands. Hickson and Parker immediately found themselves immobilized, lifted off the ground by an unseen force, and taken aboard the craft. What happened next was a blur of examinations and confusion; they had no clear sense of time. And then, just as suddenly as they had been taken, they were returned to the riverbank, shaken to their core.

When they reported the incident to the police, their terror was unmistakable. Secret recordings of their conversations revealed the deep fear they still felt. While some might dismiss their story as an elaborate hoax, others argue that something truly unexplainable occurred. And though the connection to government dealings remains tenuous, some suggest this was just the beginning of encounters that had been foreseen by those in power.

The Travis Walton Abduction: Into the Arizona Wilderness

Two years after the Pascagoula incident, another disturbing event would leave its mark on UFO lore. On November 5, 1975, Travis Walton was working in the dense forests of Arizona with his logging crew when they saw something strange hovering between the trees. A blinding light— too bright to be the setting sun—drew them closer. Suspended above the clearing was a large, metallic craft.

Ignoring the shouts of his coworkers, Walton stepped out of the truck and approached the strange object. What happened next would haunt the crewmen for years. A beam of light shot down from the craft, striking Walton and sending him flying backward. His companions, in shock, fled the scene, convinced Walton was dead.

For five days, Walton's whereabouts were a mystery. Search parties combed the forest, and police interrogated his coworkers. Then, out of nowhere, Walton reappeared, disoriented and traumatized, with a story that would captivate the world. He claimed to have been taken aboard the craft, where he encountered strange beings with large, black eyes who examined him. His story paralleled many of the UFO abduction reports that were starting to surface worldwide.

Whether Walton's experience was the result of a close encounter or an elaborate illusion, his tale remains one of the most famous in UFO history. And while skeptics have questioned its authenticity, Walton and his crew stand by their story. For those who believe in a broader conspiracy, his abduction was yet another sign that humanity had entered a new, unsettling relationship with beings from beyond—a relationship that may have been influenced by decisions made at the highest levels.

The Ariel School Incident: A Message from the Stars

Fast-forward nearly two decades to September 16, 1994. In the small rural community of Ruwa, Zimbabwe, a group of schoolchildren were enjoying their morning recess. It was an ordinary day until something extraordinary happened. A group of silver, disc-shaped objects appeared in the sky above Ariel School, hovering silently before descending just beyond the playground.

The children, numbering more than sixty, were mesmerized as they watched the craft land. What happened next was beyond their comprehension: Small beings emerged from the craft—humanoid in shape, but with large, almond-shaped eyes. The beings, the children said, communicated with them telepathically, warning of environmental destruction and the dangers of technology. The message was clear: Humanity was on a dangerous path.

When the children ran to tell their teachers, their stories were eerily consistent. The encounter left many of the children shaken, their drawings and accounts aligning in ways that were difficult to dismiss. The incident garnered immediate international attention, but the involvement of one investigator—Harvard psychiatrist Dr. John Mack—helped legitimize the case further.

Dr. Mack, known for his controversial research into alien abductions, was drawn to the incident because of the sincerity of the children's testimonies. Having previously worked with dozens of alleged abductees, Mack was no stranger to the emotional and psychological effects such experiences could have on witnesses. However, what made this case unique was the consistency of the accounts across a large group of children, each telling a remarkably similar story about what they had seen and experienced.

Mack traveled to Zimbabwe to interview the children directly. He conducted multiple sessions with them, documenting in detail their descriptions and emotional responses. What struck Mack most was how deeply affected the children were by their encounter. They spoke not only of the beings they had seen, but of the message they had received—a message that warned of humanity's destructive path and the need to change course before it was too late.

Mack's psychological expertise allowed him to assess the children for signs of fabrication or suggestibility. His conclusion? These children were not lying. He believed they had experienced something profound, something that challenged conventional understandings of reality. Though the Ariel School incident remains unproven by hard evidence, Mack's involvement lent credibility to the witnesses' experiences, making this one of the most compelling UFO sightings in modern history.

For Mack, the case reinforced his belief that these encounters weren't simply hallucinations or dreams. They were real experiences that had a deep impact on those who witnessed them, experiences that couldn't be easily explained or dismissed. His work in Zimbabwe cemented the Ariel School incident as a landmark event in the study of extraterrestrial encounters.

Betty and Barney Hill: The First Abduction of Its Kind

Before these well-known encounters, another story captured the public's imagination and laid the foundation for modern UFO abduction lore. On the night of September 19, 1961, Betty and Barney Hill were driving through the White Mountains of New Hampshire when they experienced something that would change their lives forever.

As they drove along the winding, empty road, they noticed a bright light following them in the sky. At first, they assumed it was an airplane, but the light grew larger and closer. It wasn't long before they realized it was no conventional aircraft. Panic set in as the light seemed to chase them, darting and hovering in ways that defied logic.

Barney pulled over and, with binoculars, observed strange, humanoid figures inside the craft. Terrified, he rushed back to the car, and the couple sped away. However, their attempt to escape was futile. The next thing they knew, they were in a strange fog, and two hours had passed— time they couldn't account for.

Over the following weeks, Betty began having strange dreams of being examined by beings with large eyes and strange medical equipment. As their mental and emotional stress mounted, the Hills sought help from a psychiatrist, who placed them under hypnosis. Under a trance, both Betty and Barney recalled being taken aboard a spacecraft, where they were subjected to examinations by beings they later described as "Greys."

Their story, though controversial, became the first widely publicized alien-abduction case in the United States, laying the groundwork for future reports of UFO encounters. Skeptics questioned the veracity of their account, but for many believers, the Hill abduction marked the beginning of humanity's direct contact with extraterrestrial visitors.

The Chris Bledsoe Story: A Modern-Day Encounter

In the book *UFO of God*, Chris Bledsoe recounts his early encounters with unexplained phenomena that profoundly changed his life. The following is a summary of his claims.[51]

Two weeks after Christmas, on January 8, 2007, Chris Bledsoe's life was about to change forever. It wasn't just another day—though it started off as one. Chris was burdened with depression, consumed by the failures of his business, and feeling the weight of supporting his family. His son Junior had sacrificed his education to help him with a framing job, and while they had just gotten paid, Chris couldn't shake the gnawing emptiness of his future.

That Monday morning, after finishing up the job, a casual fishing trip along the Cape Fear River with a few friends seemed like a harmless way to unwind. The group piled into Chris's red Ford pickup, and they drove through fields and pine forests, heading toward a fishing spot nestled deep in the woods on land his dad's hunting club rented. For the others, it was an opportunity to blow off steam and enjoy nature. But for Chris, the outing felt more like an escape from the suffocating pressure of his collapsing life.

As they set up their fishing poles by the riverbank, Chris couldn't ignore the darkness creeping in. While the others joked and tended to the fire they built, Chris distanced himself from the group, choosing instead to wander deeper into the woods. The weight of his failures, personal and professional, bore down on him. Every tree he passed whispered the memories of better days—days when he wasn't trapped in a life he felt was slipping away. He found an old oak tree and sat beneath it, staring at the river, his thoughts racing.

Then, in the waning daylight, something changed. A strange sense of unease crept over him, beyond his usual inner turmoil. The air seemed to grow colder, and as Chris started to head back toward the group, he heard rustling in the bushes. At first, he dismissed it as a deer—this was familiar territory, after all. But as he stopped, so did the sound. When he moved again, the rustling resumed, this time with an unsettling rhythm. This wasn't a deer. This wasn't anything natural. Fear began to sink in.

Chris hurried back to the open field, feeling an unseen presence watching him from the shadows. When he finally reached the clearing, the sight that greeted him was unlike anything he had ever imagined. At the crest of the hill, two massive, fiery red-orange spheres hovered silently over the treetops. The orbs were as large as houses, swirling with strange flames, their otherworldly light defying the darkening sky. Frozen in awe, Chris' mind struggled to process the impossible sight before him. What were they? How could something so unnatural exist in this quiet part of North Carolina?

As he knelt in disbelief, a third orb appeared, descending rapidly— as if it had been watching him all along. The sudden appearance of the third sphere jolted Chris from his stupor. Panic surged through him. His son Junior and the rest of the group were down by the river, oblivious to what was unfolding above. Without another thought, Chris turned and ran toward the campfire, the glowing spheres lingering in the sky behind him. His heart raced, not just from fear, but from an overwhelming sense of dread that something beyond comprehension was about to happen.

When Chris burst into the clearing by the fire, the scene was disorienting. His truck had been moved. The large pile of wood the group had gathered had diminished to almost nothing, and the once-blazing fire had been reduced to a few weak flames. "Where have you been?" one of the men asked, his voice thick with unease. They had been searching for him for hours. But Chris couldn't comprehend that—he had only been gone for a few minutes, hadn't he?

And where was Junior?

Chris' pulse quickened. Panic set in. Junior was gone, having ventured into the woods to look for his father. The thought of his son alone in the dark forest sent Chris running back into the trees. He pushed through the underbrush, thorns tearing at his skin, but his only concern was finding his Junior. The rustling returned, this time faster, more erratic, as if something—someone—was watching him, following his every move.

At last, Chris heard a faint voice calling, and he found his son crouched in the brush, his face pale. "Where did you go? They were here! They were watching me!" Junior was frantic, his eyes wide with fear. He spoke of strange, red-eyed creatures that had paralyzed him, keeping him rooted to the spot as they played with sticks and stones, examining them as though they were conducting some strange experiment.

Chris pulled his son close, trying to calm him, though his own mind was reeling. How could this be real? What were these entities? How had they lost hours of time—without any memory of it?

Back at the fire, the other men were visibly shaken. They had seen the lights, too—nine glowing orbs that had appeared overhead, forming a circle before scattering into the sky. Three had descended across the river, lighting up the landscape with their brilliant, pulsating energy. But it wasn't just light; there had been something deeply sinister about their presence, something that didn't belong in the world they knew.

The fear that gripped the members of the group was palpable. Chris wanted to flee, but his sense of responsibility kept him grounded. He had to get the others and himself to safety, but where could they go to escape these beings? As the men piled into the truck, panic took hold, and they screamed at Chris to drive—drive anywhere, just away from the lights. He sped through the field, but no matter how fast they went, the orbs followed, keeping pace effortlessly. The terror was relentless.

Suddenly, one of the fiery orbs descended directly in front of the truck, blocking their escape. It was no longer just a glowing ball of light, but had transformed into an egg-shaped object, swirling with brilliant, crystalline patterns. It hovered in the road, emitting a dazzling, electric-white light that seemed to pulse with an otherworldly energy. Chris slammed on the brakes, but the truck slid toward the object; he was helpless.

Then, without warning, the egg-shaped craft shot into the sky, disappearing as quickly as it had appeared. The men in the truck were breathless, stunned into silence. For a moment, it seemed they might escape after all. Chris drove to a nearby mobile home, hoping the people inside might have seen what was happening. But when he and the others arrived, the house was empty. The front door stood wide open, lights on, but there was no sign of anyone. It was as though the occupants had vanished.

As Chris and the rest of his group left the area, the same lights continued to follow them, appearing and disappearing with an eerie intelligence. But what disturbed Chris most wasn't the pursuit itself—it was the profound connection he felt with the orbs. There was something deeply personal about their interaction, as if these entities knew him, understood his fears and his failures, and were showing him something beyond mere phenomena. They weren't just watching—they were communicating.

The following days brought little comfort. Junior was still dazed, and Chris himself was left grappling with what he had seen. He couldn't shake the feeling that something far greater than an ordinary UFO sighting had occurred. It was as if the fabric of reality itself had been torn apart, revealing a glimpse of something terrifying and magnificent beyond human understanding.

One evening, as the dogs barked fiercely at something in the woods, Chris knew he had to face whatever it was. Grabbing his rifle, he walked toward a Christmas tree farm nearby, where thick evergreen branches formed an impenetrable wall of needles. As he approached, a blinding light pierced the darkness, so intense that Chris had to shield his eyes. The force of the illumination was palpable, a hum of energy that vibrated through his body as though repelling him. Unable to push forward, he retreated, but not without seeing something that would forever alter him.

Two small beings stood before him, their forms faintly glowing, their eyes red and unblinking. A triangle-shaped insignia on their chests pulsed with a strange light. The encounter wasn't aggressive, but it was profound. These beings weren't here to harm; they were here with a message. And in that moment, a powerful truth was revealed to Chris: Every living thing holds value, and all life is interconnected.

Suddenly, all his years of hunting, killing, and the mistakes of his past flooded him with crushing remorse. He dropped to his knees, overwhelmed by guilt and sorrow. What had he done? How could he ever undo the harm he'd caused? The beings didn't speak, but their presence communicated something Chris would carry with him for the rest of his life: the importance of life and the need to protect it.

As quickly as they appeared, the beings vanished, leaving Chris alone in the frosty darkness. The encounter had instilled a new mission in his heart, one of compassion, protection, and understanding of the sacredness of life. No longer the man who had ventured out to fish that January day, Chris was transformed by an experience few would believe, but that had opened his eyes to a far greater reality.

What happened drew the attention of government agencies and scientific organizations alike. When word of Chris Bledsoe's encounter spread, it attracted the interest of high-level officials within NASA, the US Department of Defense, and other investigative organizations concerned with UAPs.

The events of that January night weren't taken lightly. NASA scientists began to visit Chris, eager to explore the implications of his extraordinary experience. They conducted tests, analyzing his account for psychological, physiological, and environmental factors. Their research focused on whether Chris' encounter had caused lasting changes, both in his body and in the landscape where the event took place. Radiation levels were checked, soil samples were collected, and countless hours of interviews followed as experts sought to unravel the mystery.

The US government conducted its own investigations. Chris' reports were logged among many others as part of the growing awareness of

UAP activity. Intelligence and defense agencies were particularly interested in the seeming intelligence and behavior of the orbs, as well as their effect on human consciousness. Why had Chris been chosen for this experience? What could these orbs be?

Throughout these investigations, Chris remained cooperative and determined to find answers, but he was also steadfast in his newfound spiritual convictions. Despite the intense scrutiny, no definitive explanation was ever provided, but one thing was clear: Chris Bledsoe's experience had profound implications for the scientific and defense communities. His case became one of the most widely studied and documented UAP encounters of the modern era, further cementing the belief that humanity is not alone in the universe.[52]

The Cosmic Conspiracy Unfolds

From the Pascagoula abduction to the Ariel School sighting, from Betty and Barney Hill's lost time to Chris Bledsoe's continuing encounters, each event tells a story of contact with something beyond our world. While the direct connection to Eisenhower's rumored deal with extraterrestrials remains speculative, the pattern is undeniable. Something has been happening—whether it's the continuation of a secret pact or the unfolding of a deeper, more elusive phenomenon.

These encounters leave us with more questions than answers. *Are they the result of chance, or is there a broader agenda at play,* one governments and world leaders may have been aware of for decades? Some researchers suggest Eisenhower's agreement wasn't a one-time event, but a pivotal moment that set the stage for long-term covert operations and collaborations between human authorities and extraterrestrial beings. If true, this implies that *these incidents are part of a grander strategy*, possibly one involving technological exchange, experimentation, and a reshaping of humanity's understanding of its place in the cosmos.

In light of this possibility, certain questions naturally emerge. Could the rapid advancements in technology, particularly in fields like aerospace and communication, be linked to secret extraterrestrial knowledge? Were sightings and abductions post-Eisenhower part of an agreed-upon protocol, with government agencies managing public perception while benefitting from alien intelligence? The Majestic-12 documents and the rise of shadowy defense operations lend some weight to these theories, suggesting that our understanding of human history may only be scratching the surface of a much larger cosmic narrative.

Yet, another theory points toward a more organic evolution of extraterrestrial contact—one driven not by deals between governments, but by the steady unfolding of an inevitable truth. As sightings increase and stories of abductions multiply, are we witnessing a slow disclosure process, one in which extraterrestrial civilizations are gradually making themselves known, preparing humanity for eventual open contact? Some contend that these encounters are designed not to conquer, but to guide, offering warnings about our planet's future and calling us to reconsider our relationship with nature, technology, and each other.

And what of the moral and spiritual dimensions? The transformative experiences of figures like Chris Bledsoe—who felt a profound spiritual awakening following his encounter—pose another question: Are these beings messengers, here to realign humanity's moral compass? Could they represent a force for greater cosmic harmony, urging us to evolve not just technologically but spiritually?

The mystery continues to deepen, with each story adding another layer to the enigma. What seems clear is that these events push the boundaries of what we consider possible. Their presence is reshaping human history in ways we're only beginning understand.

As we look back on these encounters, it's hard not to wonder if the truth is far more complex than we've been led to believe. Whatever the origins of these experiences, they point to one undeniable fact: *We are not alone.* And whether or not that has been known since Eisenhower's presidency, the reality of these encounters continues to ripple through history, leaving those who witness them—and those who hear their stories—forever changed.

Looking Ahead

As Dwight D. Eisenhower's presidency came to a close, he left behind not just a legacy shaped by Cold War politics and military-industrial advancements, but also a cryptic warning—one that hinted at unseen forces and hidden agendas. His alleged encounters with extraterrestrial beings and the secret pacts forged behind closed doors would reverberate through the corridors of power for decades to come, as a young John F. Kennedy would soon realize.

Chapter 6

THE SILENCED PRESIDENT AND THE CIA CONSPIRACY

As nations become corrupt and vicious, they have more need of masters.

—BENJAMIN FRANKLIN

I love the man that can smile in trouble, that can gather strength from distress, and grow brave by reflection. 'Tis the business of little minds to shrink; but he whose heart is firm, and whose conscience approves his conduct, will pursue his principles unto death.

—THOMAS PAINE

John F. Kennedy is remembered for his bold vision of space exploration, promising in 1961 that the United States would land a man on the moon before the decade ended. His famous words sparked a race to the stars, but the moon landing was only one piece of Kennedy's broader ambition to broaden the boundaries of human understanding. Beneath this public vision lay a quieter, more elusive mission—one entangled in secrecy and a growing interest in UFOs.

Kennedy's presidency, often seen through the lens of Cold War tensions, harbored a deeper, more mysterious chapter. UFOs, covert operations, and hidden agendas weren't just the musings of conspiracy theorists; they were matters Kennedy himself reportedly pursued. As he sought to open the door to the cosmos, he was also prying into the shadowy corridors of the intelligence community, seeking answers to questions that had remained unanswered far too long.

This interest in UFOs, though seldom discussed publicly, might have played a far more significant role in his presidency than history has fully acknowledged. Some even speculate that it was this quest for disclosure—his desire to share information with NASA and the Soviet Union—that set him on a collision course with deeply entrenched, secretive powers within his own government. The question remains: Could this interest have played a role in his untimely assassination?

The NATO UFO Incident of 1961: A Crisis That Haunted Kennedy

In February 1961, an alarming event reportedly took place across European airspace that left a lasting impression on President John F. Kennedy. This incident, now referred to in UFO lore as the "NATO UFO Incident," saw NATO radar systems detect fifty unidentified objects moving at high speeds. They were tracked moving from the Soviet Union toward Europe, triggering an immediate alert and concerns that this might be the start of an aerial assault.

For a brief, tense period, both the United States and the Soviet Union scrambled to respond, fearing these objects could signal the opening of a nuclear attack. However, as the situation unfolded, both sides realized that they weren't missiles or aircraft from any known military source. Their nature remained unidentified, and some suggested they could have been extraterrestrial in origin.

The objects eventually disappeared over the Norwegian Sea, leaving behind a mystery that unsettled military planners on both sides. This incident deeply affected Kennedy, who was acutely aware of how fragile peace was during the Cold War. If unidentified objects like these could so easily trigger panic, they posed a serious risk of escalating tensions between the US and the Soviet Union, particularly during an era when the threat of nuclear war was ever present.

Kennedy's awareness of this event likely informed his later push for UFO disclosure. He saw the need for transparency between the United States and the Soviet Union on matters involving unidentified aerial phenomena (and nuclear weaponry), understanding that *misidentifications* could have catastrophic consequences. Though official records of the February 1961 NATO UFO incident are sparse, UFO researchers continue to cite it as an example of how unidentified phenomena could pose real dangers—not just to national security, but to global stability. For Kennedy, the event was a stark reminder of how easily confusion over the unknown could spiral into disaster.

Operation Palladium: The Deception That Went Deeper?

In 1961, a young president took office proclaiming that "the torch had been passed to a new generation." Indeed, John F. Kennedy brought fresh ideas, but some were deeply unpopular with established government bureaucrats and the powerful military-industrial complex. One such concern was his growing interest in the secretive handling of UFO information, an issue that likely stemmed from President Eisenhower's warning about the unchecked power of the military-industrial complex in his farewell address.

Amid the tensions of the Cold War, Kennedy was navigating the precarious balance of power between the US and the Soviet Union. During his administration, a covert intelligence enterprise known as Operation Palladium was in motion. This program, designed to provoke and measure Soviet radar defenses by sending out deceptive signals, was intended to test the Soviets' response to U2 spy planes and potential bomber strikes. If war broke out, these signals could confuse Soviet defenses, making it harder for them to distinguish between real and false threats.

However, while Operation Palladium was highly classified, there is speculation that Kennedy himself was not fully briefed on it. Some researchers argue that it wasn't until Kennedy's meeting with Soviet

Premier Nikita Khrushchev at the Vienna Summit on June 4, 1961, that the American president first learned about Palladium. According to these theories, Khrushchev revealed the clandestine operation to Kennedy, who had been unaware of it until that moment. While no official records confirm this conversation, the theory has persisted in conspiracy circles.

Shortly after returning to the United States, Kennedy began investigating Operation Palladium. A leaked memo from June 28, 1961, allegedly shows that Kennedy demanded a meeting with Allen Dulles, the director of the CIA at the time. The strained relationship between Kennedy and Dulles had only worsened following the failed Bay of Pigs invasion, and by September of 1961, Dulles was removed from his position. While Kennedy's statement that he wanted to "splinter the CIA into a thousand pieces and scatter it to the wind" remains largely anecdotal, it reflects the growing distrust between the administration and the intelligence community. Kennedy's efforts to shift intelligence powers from the CIA to the newly formed Defense Intelligence Agency (DIA) under Robert McNamara were met with fierce resistance from the military-intelligence establishment.

The June 28 memo, which surfaced in 1995, reportedly revealed that Kennedy wished to discuss MJ-12 intelligence operations in the context of Cold War psychological warfare, specifically referencing Operation Palladium.[53] Though skeptics initially dismissed the memo, the declassification of the JFK files in 2022 added credibility to its claims. The declassified Allen Dulles diary entries from December 1959 to January 1962 confirm that Dulles did meet with "the President" twice on June 28, 1961, aligning with the details of the memo.[54] While the content of these meetings remains classified, their confirmation has fueled speculation about Kennedy's growing concerns regarding covert operations like Palladium.

What Kennedy may have discovered was deeply unsettling. The MJ-12 group was reportedly involved in using deceptive radar signals not just to trick the Soviets, but to obscure the UFO phenomenon from public knowledge. Kennedy's investigation into these operations is said to have heightened his determination to push for UFO disclosure, further straining his already tense relationship with the intelligence community.

The President's Demand for Disclosure

As his presidency continued, so did John F. Kennedy's quest for the truth about unidentified flying objects. On November 12, 1963—just ten days before his assassination—he issued a now-famous memo requesting classified UFO-related intelligence. His goal? To share this data with NASA for space exploration and with the Soviets to avoid any catastrophic misunderstandings that could lead to nuclear war. Speculation suggests the NATO UFO incident of 1961 was still fresh in his mind and may have shaped his requests for UFO-related data from the CIA, as well as his push to share information with NASA and the Soviets. The November 12, 1963, memo read:

> SUBJECT: Classification review of all UFO intelligence files affecting National Security
>
> As I discussed with you previously, I have initiated...and have instructed James Webb to develop a program with the Soviet Union and joint space and lunar exploration. It would be very helpful if you would have the high threat cases reviewed with the purposes of identification of bona fide as opposed to classified CIA and USAF sources. It is important that we make a clear distinction between the knowns and unknowns in the event the Soviets try to mistake our extended cooperation as a cover for intelligence gathering of their defense and space program.[55]

Kennedy's use of the term "unknowns" in the memo was particularly significant. It acknowledged that neither the US nor the Soviet Union fully understood the nature of the phenomena they were encountering. But perhaps more importantly, by pushing for the sharing of this information, Kennedy was challenging the deeply ingrained culture of secrecy within the intelligence community.

Kennedy's Fight with the CIA: Power, Secrecy, and the UFO Connection

John F. Kennedy's willingness to challenge the CIA, especially after the disastrous Bay of Pigs invasion, quickly made him a polarizing figure within the intelligence community. His decision to remove Allen Dulles from the CIA in 1961, coupled with his infamous remark about wanting to "splinter the CIA into a thousand pieces," set the stage for a contentious relationship. This animosity only grew when Kennedy began shifting intelligence responsibilities to the newly formed DIA under Robert McNamara, sparking tension with the CIA, which had grown into a powerful and relatively unchecked institution.

At the heart of this resistance was James Jesus Angleton, the CIA's head of counterintelligence. Angleton, notorious for his paranoia and deep-rooted ties to covert operations, became more than just a counterintelligence officer—he was the gatekeeper of some of the agency's most sensitive information. Angleton's role in controlling UFO-related intelligence remains a subject of speculation, with many suggesting that his obsessive need for secrecy extended to guarding knowledge about unidentified flying objects.

While evidence directly linking Angleton to UFO control is sparse, many researchers believe that MJ-12, the group supposedly responsible for UFO secrecy, worked in tandem with Angleton. His distrust of both foreign and domestic entities likely fueled his determination to prevent UFO information from leaking, making Kennedy's push for transparency a direct threat to these secret operations.

Kennedy's efforts to pull back the curtain on UFOs through memos like the one on November 12, 1963, weren't just about transparency—they were about challenging the very foundations of Cold War secrecy. By demanding the declassification and sharing of UFO-related information with NASA and the Soviet Union, Kennedy was moving against the grain of a CIA that was deeply invested in keeping these unknowns hidden, particularly in the context of national security concerns.

VICTOR MARCHETTI: A GLIMPSE INTO CIA SECRECY

Victor Marchetti, a former senior CIA officer, provides rare insight into the agency's covert practices, including its involvement with UFOs. Joining the CIA in 1955, Marchetti held various high-ranking positions, but became disillusioned with the agency by 1969. His subsequent book, *The CIA and the Cult of Intelligence* (1974), was the first to be subjected to pre-publication government censorship. The CIA initially demanded that 366 passages be removed, but after a legal battle, only 168 were redacted.

Though UFOs were not his primary focus, Marchetti made a bold claim in a 1979 article:

We have, indeed, been contacted—perhaps even visited—by extraterrestrial beings, and the U.S. government, in collusion with the other national powers of the [E]arth, is determined to keep this information from the general public.

The purpose of the international conspiracy is to maintain a workable stability among the nations of the world and for them, in turn, to retain institutional control over their respective populations. Thus, for these governments to admit that there are beings from outer space...with mentalities and technological capabilities obviously far superior to ours, could, once fully perceived by the average person, erode the foundations of the [Earth's] traditional power structure. Political and legal systems, religions, economic and social institutions could all soon become meaningless in the mind of the public. The national oligarchical establishments, even civilization as we now know it, could collapse into anarchy.

Such extreme conclusions are not necessarily valid, but they probably accurately reflect the fears of the "ruling classes" of the major nations, whose leaders (particularly those in the intelligence business) have always advocated excessive governmental secrecy as being necessary to preserve "national security."[56]

Marchetti argued that revealing extraterrestrial contact could destabilize political, religious, and social institutions, leading to widespread societal upheaval. While his commentary on UFOs was brief, his statements provide further evidence of the intelligence community's deep-rooted secrecy on the matter. This aligns with the broader themes of JFK's battles against entrenched power structures and the efforts to keep the truth about UFOs from the public.

The Burned Memo: A Smoking Gun in the JFK-UFO Conspiracy?

Among the many documents tied to the shadowy Majestic-12 conspiracy, none has captured the imagination of investigators quite like the Burned Memo. This document, half-scorched and cryptic, is believed to have narrowly escaped destruction after being rescued from a fire by a CIA counterintelligence officer clearing out the personal safe of James Jesus Angleton, the legendary head of CIA counterintelligence, after his death. What makes this document truly remarkable isn't just its survival—it's what it might reveal about President Kennedy's assassination and his possible connection to UFO disclosure.

The Burned Memo, an original carbon copy, is marked with the red-ink stamp "TOP SECRET/MJ-12" and also features a large black "CI" (denoting "counterintelligence"). Its lack of a date stamp has left some ambiguity, though UFO researchers believe it was written in the fall of 1963, shortly before Kennedy's death. The memo is believed to have been a draft from CIA Director John A. McCone (designated as MJ-1, head of the MJ-12 group) to other MJ-designated officials, referencing several code word projects, including EVIRO, PARASITE, and PARHELION. Perhaps most intriguing are the mentions of MAJESTIC and JEHOVAH (MJ), terms that suggest these were highly classified, UFO-related operations.

In the context of President Kennedy, the memo's ominous line—"Lancer's inquiries into our activities cannot be allowed"—is chilling. It states:

> In the context of the above it has become necessary to review and evaluate duplication in field activities in light of the current situation. To eliminate this problem, I have drafted new directives for your review and consideration. Please evaluate each draft on its own merit with the goal of finding acceptable solutions in which all can agree on [sic]. As you must know **LANCER [undoubtedly, President Kennedy] has made some inquiries regarding our activities which we cannot allow.** Please submit your views no later than October. Your action to this matter is critical to the continuance of the group.[57] (emphasis added)

Lancer, Kennedy's Secret Service code name, raises the question of whether his inquiries into UFO-related activities, including his November 12, 1963, memo requesting the declassification of UFO information, were seen as dangerous by those controlling MJ-12 operations. Could Kennedy's push for transparency have clashed with deeply entrenched forces who were determined to keep the UFO mystery hidden?

Further intrigue surrounds the Burned Memo's association with James Jesus Angleton, a figure who looms large in the world of counterintelligence. Angleton was known for his extreme secrecy and paranoia, making it no surprise that such sensitive material might have been in his personal safe. Angleton's ties to covert operations, combined with his close relationship with the former CIA Director Allen Dulles (whom Kennedy had fired), suggest a possible web of interconnections that may have placed the president in direct opposition to some of the most secretive factions within the US government.

Many UFO researchers, including Ryan Wood, author of Majic Eyes Only, argue that the Burned Memo represents clear evidence of a concerted effort to keep UFO-related information out of Kennedy's hands. Wood describes the memo as "the most historic" among the original MJ-12 documents, believing its contents raise serious questions about how much the US government knew about extraterrestrial technology—and what lengths it would go to in order to protect those secrets.

Yet the Burned Memo remains shrouded in controversy. Critics, including the FBI, have dismissed it, but forensic analysis of the physical document, as well as its origins in Angleton's safe, have kept believers convinced of its authenticity. In any case, this document adds another layer to the vast conspiracy theories that surround Kennedy's assassination. Was his life cut short because of his push to expose the truth about UFOs that the intelligence community had been hiding for years? Many theorists argue that his attempts to declassify UFO material were the final straw for the intelligence community. He was no longer just a political adversary—he was a threat to a covert agenda that spanned beyond Cold War politics.

Ultimately, the Burned Memo leaves more questions than answers. But for those who believe in the document's authenticity, it's a rare glimpse into the hidden machinations of Cold War-era intelligence—where UFOs, covert operations, and presidential power collided in ways that may have forever altered the course of history.

Kennedy's Final Battle: A Collision of Transparency and Secrecy

In the final weeks of his life, President Kennedy's relentless push for UFO transparency collided with the entrenched secrecy of the intelligence community. His November 12, 1963, memo, a bold request for the declassification of UFO-related intelligence, was more than just another executive order—it was a direct challenge to the covert power structures that had thrived in the shadows for decades. By advocating for sharing this sensitive information with NASA and even the Soviet Union, Kennedy was attempting to bridge an unprecedented gap—one that linked national defense with the mysteries of the unknown.

But Kennedy's moves went far beyond UFO disclosure. His broader efforts to reform the CIA—which had amassed extraordinary, unchecked power in the years following World War II—set him on a collision course with the very forces that guarded these secrets. His decision to strip power from the CIA and redistribute it to the DIA under McNamara was nothing short of revolutionary. The intelligence community, long accustomed to operating autonomously, now found itself in direct conflict with a president who wasn't afraid to dismantle the very systems that gave it its power.

Kennedy's infamous decision to remove Allen Dulles as director of the CIA in 1961, after the Bay of Pigs debacle, had already sent shockwaves through Washington. His reported desire to "splinter the CIA into a thousand pieces" left no room for doubt—Kennedy was a threat to those who operated in the shadows. As his presidency advanced, James Jesus Angleton, the shadowy head of CIA counterintelligence, became a key figure in opposing Kennedy's agenda. Angleton's paranoia and tight grip over the agency's deepest secrets—particularly its UFO files—placed him in direct conflict with the president's push for transparency.

At the heart of this struggle was Majestic-12, the secretive group believed to be responsible for controlling the government's UFO knowledge. Many researchers contend that Angleton and MJ-12 worked in tandem to keep this information tightly controlled. As Kennedy's inquiries into these matters became more pointed, the tension escalated, creating an explosive situation behind the scenes.

The critical question remains: Had Kennedy succeeded in his quest for UFO disclosure, what would the world have learned? Would his revelations have upended not only the Cold War power balance but also our understanding of its place in the cosmos? These questions remain unanswered, shrouded in layers of classified documents and decades of speculation.

What is clear, however, is that Kennedy was on the verge of revealing far more than just Cold War secrets. His efforts to unlock the truth about humanity's encounters with the unknown were gaining momentum, and the November 12 memo was likely just the start. The evidence suggests Kennedy's assassination may have been about more than political power or Cold War rivalries. It may have centered around the control of secrets far beyond our world—secrets that, if revealed, could have reshaped humankind's understanding of the cosmos.

Looking Ahead

The hidden conflict between transparency and secrecy, between discovery and deception, continues to shape the world we live in today. And as we turn our eyes to space, the question remains: How much of the truth has been withheld, and at what cost?

In the next chapter, we will explore the presidents who followed Kennedy and their quest to unlock the mysteries of space. Were their administrations merely caretakers of these cosmic secrets, or did they delve deeper into the search for extraterrestrial intelligence? As humanity expanded its reach into the stars, the battle for the truth would only intensify.

Chapter 7

THE SPACE PRESIDENTS AND THE SEARCH FOR EXTRATERRESTRIAL LIFE

> Astronomers tell us, with good reason, that not only all the
> planets and satellites in our solar system are inhabited, but
> all the unnumbered worlds that revolve around the fixed
> stars are inhabited.
>
> —JOHN ADAMS

Lyndon B. Johnson: Architect of the Space Age

For centuries, humanity has gazed up at the stars, wondering if we are truly alone in the vast expanse of the universe. While our imaginations have often conjured up ideas of life beyond Earth, the term "extraterrestrial" carries with it more than just speculation. It signifies the possibility of life from other planets—beings that might exist in realms far beyond our solar system, and perhaps even closer than we think. As we continue to advance in space exploration, the questions surrounding extraterrestrial life grow more pressing.

President Lyndon B. Johnson navigated the rapidly shifting landscape of space exploration and the emerging discourse on unidentified flying objects. His role in advancing NASA's achievements, most notably paving the way for the Apollo missions, is well documented. Yet, his presidency is also marked by a more clandestine chapter, involving the growing secrecy surrounding UFOs and the potential existence of extraterrestrial life. From unexplained incidents to the rise of military-industrial control over UFO investigations, Johnson's era set the stage for the intrigue and speculation that would follow under future presidents.

As we journey through this pivotal moment in American history, we will delve into the delicate balance between space triumphs and the shadowy undercurrent of UFO mysteries—asking not just what Johnson's administration accomplished, but also what may have been left unsaid.

Lyndon B. Johnson: UFO Skeptic?

Lyndon B. Johnson's presidency is deeply tied to America's achievements in space exploration, but there is a lesser-known chapter involving UFO phenomena and the executive branch's shifting role in overseeing these secrets. From his days as Senate majority leader, Johnson saw space not merely as a domain for exploration, but as a geopolitical battleground. The launch of Sputnik 1 in 1957 had rattled the United States, creating fear that the Soviet Union might control space—and, by extension, dominate the Earth. Johnson, recognizing the strategic implications, pushed hard to create the National Aeronautics and Space Act of 1958, which established NASA. As the force behind NASA's move to Houston, Johnson made space his personal priority both as vice president under Kennedy and later as president.

However, as Johnson advanced the American space agenda, the era was also marked by significant UFO-related incidents, leaving some to wonder whether he had a more covert interest in UFO phenomena. During his tenure, several notable UFO cases, including the Kecksburg incident and the Malmstrom ICBM shutdown, fueled public intrigue, yet Johnson himself remained tight-lipped on the issue. The true nature of his views on extraterrestrial life remains shrouded in ambiguity, leaving room for speculation about how deeply UFOs intersected with his presidency.

Cold War Space Race: Johnson's Strategic Role

For Johnson, space exploration wasn't just about technological superiority—it was about national security. His commitment to space exploration, born out of the Cold War rivalry with the Soviet Union, was central to his legacy. By leveraging his Senate leadership, Johnson spearheaded efforts to secure funding and support for NASA. His rhetoric, amplified by Democratic strategist George Reedy, suggested that control of space meant control of the world, a sentiment that positioned the United States for a head-to-head race with the Soviets.

However, Johnson's enthusiasm for space was tempered by a complex landscape of defense priorities. As the Vietnam War dragged on, his administration faced budgetary constraints, leading to the Outer Space Treaty of 1967, which curtailed some of the most expensive space projects. This diplomatic achievement sought to ensure that space remained a neutral zone, free from the threat of weaponization, but it also symbolized a reduction in space-related ambitions.

The Condon Report: A Blow to UFO Research

Johnson's presidency also coincided with the era of the Condon Report, a government-sanctioned study into UFOs that fundamentally shaped public perception of the phenomenon. In 1966, following years of increasing UFO sightings and public pressure, the Air Force commissioned the University of Colorado, under the direction of physicist Edward Condon, to evaluate the UFO phenomenon. Despite the report's conclusion that UFOs did not pose a threat to national security, the findings were criticized as biased, especially by figures like Donald Keyhoe and Dr. James E. McDonald, who believed the government was concealing critical UFO information. Keyhoe, the outspoken head of the National Investigations Committee on Aerial Phenomena, famously wrote to Johnson condemning the Condon Report's methodology and accusing the government of whitewashing the UFO issue.

For Johnson, the Condon Report offered a convenient resolution to the mounting UFO speculation. By accepting its findings, he could divert attention away from further UFO investigations and focus on the space race's more immediate and visible achievements. Yet, as Keyhoe's letter indicated, powerful forces were at play within the military-industrial complex and intelligence community, who might have sought to maintain secrecy around the UFO issue, even as public interest intensified.

Johnson's Strained Power over UFOs: The Intelligence Shift

While Johnson wielded immense influence in space exploration, the era also marked a subtle but significant shift of power regarding UFO secrecy. In contrast to earlier administrations, where the executive branch retained some oversight of UFO investigations, the growing influence of military and intelligence entities, particularly the Air Force, began to eclipse presidential control. By the time of Johnson's presidency, UFO-related matters had become increasingly shielded from civilian oversight. Many researchers suggest this growing secrecy, combined with the military-industrial complex's desire to protect sensitive technologies, may have led to the president being excluded from access to critical UFO knowledge.

This shift is particularly intriguing when examining UFO incidents like Kecksburg and the Malmstrom ICBM shutdown. Despite these high-profile cases occurring during his administration, there is little evidence that Johnson was actively involved in their investigation or resolution. Some conspiracy theorists argue that this lack of involvement wasn't due to disinterest, but rather was the result of a concerted effort to exclude the president from sensitive UFO information.

Conspiracies and Balance: What Did Johnson Really Know?

Balancing conspiratorial narratives with historical fact is essential when investigating Lyndon B. Johnson's role in space and UFO matters.

While he was undoubtedly instrumental in advancing America's space program, the extent of his involvement in UFO phenomena is far murkier. The Donald Keyhoe letter and Condon Report are emblematic of the tensions between public curiosity and government secrecy during this period. The intelligence community's growing control over UFO research left Johnson with little direct influence over these matters, even though UFO-related incidents continued to occur under his watch.

While Johnson may not have been deeply involved in UFO cover-ups, his administration's focus on space exploration paved the way for future presidencies to engage with the topic in both overt and covert ways. The unanswered questions surrounding UFOs during his time remain a testament to the shadowy interplay of power, secrecy, and the unknown that characterized the Cold War era.

The Shifting Tides of Space and Secrecy

With Johnson's departure from office, a new chapter in space exploration and UFO secrecy began. The transition from his presidency to those of Richard Nixon, Ronald Reagan, George H. W. Bush, and beyond marked a subtle but profound shift in both public and clandestine space initiatives. While Johnson laid the foundation for NASA's crowning achievements, such as the Apollo moon landing, he also presided over the rise of an intelligence apparatus that increasingly kept UFO matters out of presidential reach. This tightening grip would define the administrations that followed, wherein space exploration became as much a geopolitical tool as a frontier for possible extraterrestrial engagement. Each president, starting with Nixon, would navigate these murky waters—balancing public triumphs with the growing weight of secrecy about what truly lay beyond Earth's atmosphere. The following sections will flesh this out.

Richard Nixon (1969-1974): The Lunar Legacy President

Richard Nixon's presidency is often remembered for the Apollo 11 moon landing in 1969, a triumph that fulfilled John F. Kennedy's bold vision of placing a man on the moon. But behind the grandeur of this achievement was a more shadowy, lesser-known dimension to Nixon's space legacy—a domain where the lines between public achievement and hidden agendas blurred.

Nixon wasn't just a passive observer of NASA's success; he actively shaped the direction of US space policy during his time in office. Beyond celebrating the moon landing, Nixon played a role in the winding down of manned lunar exploration. Budget cuts, shifting national priorities, and, some argue, secret military interests diverted funds from the ambitious space race to other arenas. While publicly supportive of NASA, Nixon quietly oversaw the transition from the Apollo missions to the Space Shuttle Program—an initiative some suggest had more military applications than civilian ones.

What remains unclear is whether Nixon, embroiled in the geopolitical tensions of the Cold War, saw the potential for space not just as a domain for exploration, but also as a theater for extraterrestrial defense. Did the Space Shuttle Program, with its promise of reusable spacecraft, serve as a cover for a more covert agenda involving surveillance of potential alien threats? The military applications of space technology, under Nixon's administration, seemed to become more prominent, but the full extent of this agenda remains hidden behind layers of secrecy. In the next chapter, we will explore in depth how President Nixon intersects with the UFO phenomenon.

Jimmy Carter (1977–1981): The Shuttle President

Jimmy Carter's presidency isn't widely associated with major space initiatives, especially when compared to the landmark efforts of his predecessors and successors. Kennedy pushed America to the moon, Nixon started the space shuttle program, and Reagan spearheaded the Strategic Defense Initiative (SDI). Carter, by contrast, didn't propose any significant new space projects, and his administration's space policy seemed more restrained. However, despite this, Carter's influence on

NASA's Space Shuttle Program proved crucial at a moment when it was in jeopardy.

In 1978, the Carter administration issued its space policy directive, Presidential Directive/NSC 37. Although it outlined broad goals like maintaining US leadership in space science and technology, the order lacked specific proposals or new missions, reflecting Carter's more cautious approach to space. His focus on budget constraints and a preference for robotic exploration over human spaceflight set him apart from earlier administrations.

However, behind the scenes, Carter played an unexpected and pivotal role in keeping NASA's Space Shuttle Program alive. According to NASA's then administrator, Robert Frosch, the program was facing severe budget shortfalls, threatening to derail plans for its development. Frosch presented Carter with the bleak reality: NASA couldn't meet the Space Shuttle's flight schedule with the funds it had. Carter, despite his lack of enthusiasm for human spaceflight, responded with an unexpected question: "How much do you need?"[58]

Carter's decision to back the Space Shuttle Program, despite his personal reservations and Vice President Walter Mondale's opposition, proved vital. Carter understood the shuttle's importance for national security, particularly for launching military satellites. His financial support ensured the shuttle's continuation, cementing his legacy as the president who saved American human spaceflight at a critical moment. Though Carter's space legacy may not be as high profile as others, the shuttle's success in the following decades owes much to his timely intervention.

Carter and UFO Secrecy: The Untold Story

Beyond his role in the Space Shuttle Program, Jimmy Carter's presidency remains uniquely intertwined with the UFO phenomenon. Carter is the only modern US president to have personally filed a UFO sighting report. The event occurred in 1969, before he became governor of Georgia, when he and a group of men witnessed an unexplained bright light in the sky during a Lions Club meeting in Leary, Georgia. Carter recounted how the object changed colors—white to blue to red—before it receded into the distance. He said:

> And all of a sudden one of the men said, "Look over to the west!" And there was a bright light in the sky. We all saw it. And then the light got closer to us. And then it stopped, I don't know how far away, but it stopped beyond the pine trees. And all of a sudden it changed color to blue, and then it changed to red, and then back to white. We were all trying to figure out what in the world it could be, and then it receded into the distance.[59]

As an amateur astronomer, Carter was certain that what he saw wasn't Venus, the planet commonly cited as the culprit in UFO sightings. For years after the event, Carter continued to describe the object as a "UFO," although he maintained that it likely had a terrestrial explanation.

Carter's UFO sighting sparked public expectations that, if elected president, he would disclose government-held information about UFOs. During his campaign, Carter promised transparency, vowing to release any documents related to UFOs. However, once in office, this promise quietly faded. Conspiracy theories emerged, with many suggesting Carter was obstructed by powerful forces within the intelligence community. One rumor alleged that CIA Director George H. W. Bush told Carter that even as president, he didn't have the "need to know" about certain classified UFO information.

Undeterred, Carter is said to have explored alternative routes for obtaining the truth. According to some accounts, he instructed the Congressional Research Service (CRS) to investigate extraterrestrial intelligence. Marcia Smith, a CRS analyst, was tasked with compiling a report on UFOs, and this is where Daniel Sheehan, a prominent lawyer (graduate of Harvard Law School) and activist, entered the story. In 1977 Sheehan was general counsel to the United States Jesuit National Headquarters. Sheehan's involvement would soon become one of the most contentious elements of Carter's alleged efforts to uncover UFO secrets.

Sheehan recounted that while assisting Smith, he requested access to classified Project Blue Book files, the official Air Force investigation into UFOs that had closed in 1969. What followed, according to Sheehan, was an extraordinary series of events that would shake his understanding of what the government knew about UFOs.

Sheehan claimed he was granted access to a highly secure vault within the Library of Congress, where he encountered microfilm that contained shocking images. As he scrolled through the film, he came across a series of photographs that appeared to depict a crashed disc-shaped craft, approximately 30 feet in diameter, embedded in the side of a hill at a 30-degree angle, surrounded by snow. It featured unusual symbols on the lower section of the upper dome, resembling a mix between cuneiform and mathematical notations. Four military personnel—likely from the Air Force—stood nearby, wearing winter parkas with fur-lined hoods, taking measurements and documenting the scene. Three men had still cameras, while a fourth held a vintage shoulder-mounted (double-reel) motion film camera, suggesting the crash occurred between 1948 and 1961.[60] The craft, Sheehan noted, had no visible seams or rivets, and its sleek, metallic surface suggested technology far beyond anything he had ever seen.

In a daring move, Sheehan claimed he had sketched the images on the cardboard backing of his legal pad. Despite the intense security, he managed to sneak these sketches out of the vault. These drawings, he believed, were irrefutable evidence of the government's involvement in UFO retrieval operations. To Sheehan, this moment was a revelation—a glimpse into the covert operations that had been kept hidden from the public eye for decades.

Despite what he had seen, Sheehan realized such information was guarded by an impenetrable wall of secrecy. Even the president, who had promised UFO transparency, appeared to be struggling against the entrenched intelligence apparatus. Sheehan later reflected that this vault of hidden knowledge wasn't just a physical barrier, but a symbol of the deeper struggle for truth in the face of government control.

Sheehan's revelations, if true, were significant. He claimed the information he had gathered was relayed to Marcia Smith, who then incorporated it into two reports for President Carter. The first allegedly stated there were between two and six highly advanced extraterrestrial civilizations within the Milky Way galaxy. The second report suggested the US Air Force was certain a significant number of UFO sightings were indeed extraterrestrial craft visiting Earth. These reports, however, were never publicly confirmed, and Carter, despite his initial enthusiasm for UFO transparency, remained conspicuously silent on the issue.

The emotional weight of Sheehan's story cannot be overlooked. He had ventured into a realm few outsiders had ever glimpsed, only to come face to face with a reality that was both astonishing and deeply frustrating. The secrecy was suffocating, and the knowledge that such monumental information was locked away—perhaps forever—left Sheehan with a sense of powerlessness. He had touched the truth, but, like so many before him, he was unable to bring it to light.

Even more telling is the effect this might have had on President Carter himself. By all accounts, Carter entered office with genuine curiosity and a desire to lift the veil of secrecy surrounding UFOs. But by the time he left the White House, that curiosity had been subdued, possibly by the same forces that had frustrated Sheehan. The promise of disclosure had faded into silence, leaving behind a lingering question: Had Carter learned something so profound that it justified the continued secrecy? Or had he, like Sheehan, been thwarted by a government apparatus determined to control the flow of information?

Remarkably, despite the frustrations of his experience during the Carter presidency, Sheehan remains an active force in the ongoing UAP disclosure movement today. His belief that the public deserves to know the truth about extraterrestrial encounters has never waned. In recent years, Sheehan has represented key whistleblowers, including Luis Elizondo, the former head of the Pentagon's Advanced Aerospace Threat

Identification Program (AATIP). Elizondo has become one of the most prominent figures pushing for transparency about UAPs, and Sheehan's legal expertise has been central in protecting whistleblowers and advocating for the release of classified information.

Sheehan's continued involvement in modern UAP disclosure efforts demonstrates how the questions of secrecy and control he encountered during the Carter era remain relevant today. His advocacy, both in the courtroom and in public discourse, keeps the pressure on the US government to come clean about what it knows regarding UFOs. As the UAP issue gains more mainstream attention, Sheehan's work stands as a testament to his enduring commitment to unravel the truth behind the phenomena.

Ronald Reagan (1981–1989): The Star Wars President

Ronald Reagan's presidency marked a pivotal shift in US space policy, ushering in a more militarized approach with the announcement of the Strategic Defense Initiative (SDI), famously dubbed "Star Wars." On the surface, SDI was a missile defense system designed to protect the United States from nuclear attacks, employing space-based interceptors to neutralize incoming warheads. However, beneath this public narrative lay a more enigmatic focus—one that conspiracy theorists and ufologists believe was directed toward extraterrestrial threats. Reagan's repeated references to the potential for an "alien threat" raised eyebrows, leading many to speculate that SDI may have been part of a covert plan to defend against more than just Soviet missiles.

During the same era, the scientific community formalized its efforts to search for extraterrestrial intelligence with the establishment of the SETI (Search for Extraterrestrial Intelligence) Institute in 1984. While the broader SETI had been underway since the 1960s, the creation of the organization marked a pivotal moment in organizing and advancing the academic pursuit of detecting potential signals from alien civilizations. In contrast to the SDI, which focused on national defense, SETI's mission was purely scientific and peaceful, aiming to explore humanity's place in the cosmos by scanning the skies for signs of intelligent life.

Though distinct from government defense programs like SDI, some have speculated that the timing of SETI's formalization alongside SDI suggests parallel paths—one focused on communication and discovery, the other on potential defense. While there is no official evidence linking SETI and SDI, both arose during a period of heightened curiosity about extraterrestrial phenomena. Reagan's administration, with its interest in both space defense and extraterrestrial life, fostered a climate wherein both scientific exploration and military preparedness were at the forefront of national policy. SETI, however, remained firmly rooted in the academic realm, far from the militarized focus of SDI. Although no direct link between SDI and SETI existed, Reagan's presidency was marked by a growing interest in the possibility of extraterrestrial life, with scientific and defense institutions pushing boundaries in their respective domains.

Reagan's fascination with UFOs and extraterrestrial life wasn't a well-kept secret. In fact, it was largely fueled by two personal UFO sightings he experienced prior to taking office. One of the most notable occurred in 1974, when Reagan was governor of California. While aboard a Cessna Citation, Reagan and his pilot, Bill Paynter, observed a mysterious light that followed their plane before abruptly accelerating into the sky at an angle and speed unlike anything known at the time. Paynter later remarked that, after witnessing such a phenomenon, it would be hard for anyone to deny the existence of UFOs. Though Reagan never spoke publicly about the incident, it solidified his personal intrigue with the UFO phenomenon.

His fascination only deepened when he became president, as he had access to classified intelligence briefings, including those conducted by then CIA Director William Casey. Some conspiracy theorists suggest these briefings included information on UFO-related matters, with Reagan being privy to secrets denied to his predecessors. This claim was bolstered by Reagan's close relationships with figures in intelligence and defense, with whom discussions on extraterrestrial issues allegedly took place.

Perhaps the most striking public evidence of Reagan's thoughts on extraterrestrials came during a speech he delivered to the United Nations General Assembly on September 21, 1987. In an unscripted moment, Reagan mused:

> In our obsession with antagonisms of the moment, we often forget how much unites all the members of humanity. Perhaps we need some outside, universal threat to make us recognize this common bond. I occasionally think how quickly our differences worldwide would vanish if we were facing an alien threat from outside this world. And yet, I ask you, is not an alien force already among us?[61]

This speech sparked widespread curiosity and speculation. Was Reagan merely using a hypothetical scenario to emphasize global unity, or was he alluding to classified information that suggested a real extraterrestrial presence? Reagan's frequent allusions to an "alien threat" during his presidency led many to wonder if he was hinting at something more than just rhetorical musings.

Some conspiracy theorists suggest SDI wasn't merely a shield against nuclear missiles, but was also a first step toward creating a defense system against extraterrestrial threats. While this theory remains speculative, intriguing threads lend credence to the idea. Reagan's strategic advisors, including Edward Teller, one of the most prominent physicists behind the development of the hydrogen bomb, were enthusiastic proponents of SDI. Teller's interest in advanced space technologies and defense led to speculation that the initiative might have been a precursor to something more secretive—a shield not just for Cold War adversaries, but for defending Earth against extraterrestrial forces.

The connection between Reagan's space policy and his interest in UFOs is further complicated by stories circulating in ufologist circles.

One of the most bizarre involves actress Shirley MacLaine, who claimed Reagan once had a close encounter with a UFO while on his way to a Hollywood party. According to MacLaine, Reagan and his wife, Nancy, encountered a UFO blocking their car. As the story goes, an alien being supposedly telepathically instructed Reagan to "leave acting and go into politics." While the story is widely considered a fabrication, Reagan's friends and family have consistently noted his genuine interest in UFOs, further adding layers to his enigmatic presidency.

Another speculative narrative centers around a supposed CIA briefing to Reagan early in his administration. Allegedly, Reagan was briefed on the 1947 Roswell incident by an insider known only as the "Caretaker," who reportedly oversaw all UFO-related matters within the CIA. According to this account, the briefing included details about crashed extraterrestrial spacecraft, recovered alien bodies, and ongoing contact with various extraterrestrial races. Though the authenticity of this account remains highly dubious, it nonetheless stokes the conspiracy theories surrounding Reagan's involvement in UFO matters.

The increasing militarization of space under Reagan wasn't limited to SDI, however. His administration also laid the groundwork for private space exploration, helping move the space race from a strictly governmental endeavor to one that invited commercial entities. This shift in policy allowed companies like SpaceX and Blue Origin to thrive in a competitive space economy. Yet even in this expansion, some suggest private-sector involvement may not be entirely separated from government projects related to UFO research. Some theorists believe that behind the public facade of commercial space exploration lies classified information and hidden agendas—perhaps linked to a broader extraterrestrial narrative.

The 1986 Japan Air Lines Flight 1628 incident offers further fuel for speculation. While flying over Alaska, the crew of a Boeing 747 witnessed several unidentified flying objects that seemed to track their plane. Captain Kenju Terauchi described the objects as massive—some as large as an aircraft carrier. Radar operators at nearby Elmendorf Air

Force Base detected unusual readings during the event, and the FAA began an investigation. Though the incident was downplayed by the government, some in Reagan's administration reportedly took an interest, raising the possibility that the president himself may have been briefed on the encounter. This event, along with Reagan's interest in extraterrestrial matters, seems to suggest that UFO phenomena were more than just a passing curiosity for his administration.

Reagan's remarks about UFOs and the possibility of alien life continue to captivate both scholars and conspiracy theorists. Was SDI simply a means of deterrence during the Cold War, or was there a deeper, hidden agenda aimed at defending against otherworldly threats? Did Reagan's curiosity about UFOs influence his policies, or were his remarks mere speculation about the nature of human existence in the universe?

While we may never have definitive answers, it's clear that Reagan's presidency—marked by a growing concern for space defense and his frequent musings on extraterrestrial life—continues to shape the narrative around UFOs, extraterrestrial intelligence, and space policy. Reagan's tenure may ultimately be remembered not just for its Cold War legacy, but also for the enduring mystery of what he truly believed about life beyond Earth.

George H. W. Bush (1989–1993): The Mars Dreamer and CIA President

George H. W. Bush's tenure as president saw the unveiling of the ambitious Space Exploration Initiative (SEI), a plan to return humans to the moon and eventually send them to Mars. On the surface, this seemed like a logical continuation of America's leadership in space exploration. But could other motivations have been driving Bush's Mars ambitions?

Bush, like his predecessors, had ties to the intelligence community, having served as director of the CIA. His administration's unveiling of SEI came at a time when the Cold War was winding down, and many wonder whether there was a deeper geopolitical—or even extraterrestrial—motive behind the Mars initiative. Was Bush aware of something beyond mere scientific curiosity? Some UFO researchers point to a potential connection between the push for Mars exploration and rumored discoveries of extraterrestrial artifacts either on the moon or on Mars itself.

Bush's ties to the intelligence community and his administration's silence on UFO-related matters, such as the continued secrecy surrounding the Roswell incident, lead some to speculate that the Mars initiative wasn't just about exploration, but about uncovering ancient extraterrestrial technology. While SEI failed to gain the necessary political or financial backing, the vision it laid out would inspire future administrations and keep the dream of Mars alive. More will be said about George H. W. Bush in another chapter.

Bill Clinton (1993-2001): The Space Station President

When Bill Clinton assumed office in 1993, his presidency was marked by a unique blend of curiosity, particularly about space and UFO phenomena. Clinton, like Jimmy Carter before him, entered the White House with a deep personal interest in uncovering the mysteries surrounding extraterrestrial life and government secrets. Yet, despite his efforts, he found himself thwarted by a system deeply entrenched in secrecy.

Clinton's curiosity extended into the vast expanse of space, but his ambitions there were tempered by the post-Cold War geopolitical climate. One of his key achievements in space diplomacy was the expansion of the International Space Station (ISS), in which he played a pivotal role in bringing Russia on board. By fostering cooperation between the US and Russia on the ISS in 1993, Clinton transformed what was initially a Cold War battleground into a platform for scientific collaboration. This partnership was more than just a scientific endeavor; it was a diplomatic victory in using space as a tool for reconciliation between former superpower adversaries.

Clinton's presidency also oversaw NASA's continued exploration efforts, most notably the Mars Pathfinder mission in 1997. These missions reflected his administration's push to ensure American leadership in space science. Yet, in tandem with these space advancements, Clinton harbored a more personal quest: the search for truth about UFOs.

A Search for UFO Truths, but Blocked by Secrecy

Bill Clinton's early interest in UFOs became public when he tasked Assistant Attorney General Webster Hubble with investigating two major mysteries—who killed John F. Kennedy and what the government knew about UFOs. Clinton wanted answers, but Hubble's search led to dead ends. The efforts only emphasized the labyrinthine walls of secrecy surrounding the topics.

To combat government opacity, Clinton signed Executive Order 12958 in 1995, declassifying millions of historical documents. While this effort led to the release of numerous Cold War and Vietnam-era records, it conspicuously left out the most anticipated UFO-related files. Clinton's chief of staff, John Podesta, was instrumental in promoting this declassification, but the secrecy around extraterrestrial matters remained intact. Clinton's frustration with this veil of secrecy was palpable, and his public comments throughout his presidency offered insights into his struggles.

In November 1995, while giving a speech in Belfast, Northern Ireland, Clinton humorously responded to a young boy's question about the Roswell incident: "No, as far as I know," Clinton said, "an alien spacecraft did not crash in Roswell, New Mexico, in 1947. And Ryan, if the United States Air Force did recover alien bodies, they didn't tell me about it either, and I want to know." Although delivered with a smile, this response contained an implicit message: Even the president might not have access to the truth about certain government secrets.

Years later, in a 2014 interview for the documentary *The Phenomenon*, Clinton was more candid about his failed attempts to unlock the mystery:

> I did attempt to discover if there were any secret government documents that reveal things, and if there were, they were concealed from me too. I wouldn't be the first president that underlings

had lied to or career bureaucrats have waited out. There may be some career person sitting around somewhere hiding these dark secrets even from elected presidents, but if so they successfully eluded me, and I am almost embarrassed to tell you I did try to find out.[62]

This startling admission reinforced the idea that career officials and entrenched bureaucracies might be guarding sensitive UFO information from even the highest levels of government. Clinton's words echo the suspicions that past presidents—Carter, for instance—shared: Some knowledge is simply beyond their reach.

The Rockefeller Initiative: The Push for UFO Disclosure

Adding complexity to Clinton's UFO narrative was his involvement with Laurance Rockefeller, a billionaire passionate about UFO disclosure. The Rockefeller Initiative, as it came to be known, saw Rockefeller lobbying the Clinton administration throughout the 1990s to release UFO-related documents. Both Bill and Hillary Clinton met with Rockefeller, most notably at his JY Ranch in Jackson Hole, Wyoming, where discussions about UFO amnesty and the release of classified information likely occurred.

Although Rockefeller's efforts were well documented in Clinton Presidential Library archives, they bore little fruit. Clinton seemed patronizing in his dealings with Rockefeller, and despite the support of UFO researchers funded by the initiative, the president's public actions showed no strong commitment to furthering UFO disclosure. Many believe that while Clinton was genuinely curious, he faced resistance from an intricate web of military and intelligence officials who held the keys to these extraterrestrial secrets.

Clinton's Lingering Questions

Even after leaving office, Clinton's curiosity about UFOs remained. During a 2021 appearance on the ABC talk show *Live with Kelly and*

Mark, he made a telling comment about the government's continued uncertainty surrounding the phenomenon: "There are things flying around out there that we haven't fully identified yet."[63] This acknowledgment, decades after his presidency, added fuel to the ongoing debate about the US government's knowledge—or lack thereof—of unidentified aerial phenomena.

Clinton's journey as president reflects the broader struggle for transparency within the government's most sensitive domains. His efforts to maintain US leadership in space were largely successful, marked by international collaboration and key Mars missions. However, when it came to UFOs, Clinton found himself hitting the same brick walls that had stymied previous presidents, leading to more questions than answers.

Barack Obama (2009–2017): The Private Space Innovator

Barack Obama's presidency marked a dramatic shift in space policy, with a heavy emphasis on partnerships with private companies. His administration fostered the rise of companies like SpaceX and Blue Origin, which now play a pivotal role in the future of space exploration. But beneath this shift toward privatization, some believe there may be deeper, more secretive motives at play.

Obama's decision to pivot away from lunar exploration and focus on Mars missions raised questions among space enthusiasts and conspiracy theorists alike. Why the sudden shift away from the moon? Some speculate that Obama's administration may have been privy to classified knowledge about extraterrestrial artifacts or even hidden bases on the lunar surface. Could this have been the reason for the sudden change in direction? Was the shift to Mars a strategic move to divert attention from possible discoveries already made on the moon?

During his tenure, NASA redirected its long-term mission toward Mars, focusing on deep-space exploration while simultaneously cutting short plans for returning astronauts to the lunar surface. This decision puzzled many, especially given the public's historical fascination with the moon and the fact that earlier space missions had laid the groundwork for further lunar exploration. Obama's administration, however, framed this decision as looking toward the future, emphasizing the potential for Mars as a human settlement. Still, conspiracy theorists couldn't help but wonder: Was there something on the moon that prompted the government to quietly shift its gaze toward the Red Planet?

More intriguingly, Obama's aggressive push toward privatization in space exploration has sparked its own set of theories. By fostering private-sector involvement in space missions, some argue that the administration may have used these companies to conduct covert operations—missions that would otherwise be too risky or controversial for a government-run program. SpaceX, led by Elon Musk, was frequently at the forefront of these missions, launching spacecraft into deep space and even aiming to reach Mars. Could these missions have had a dual purpose? Were they not only about advancing human space exploration, but also about serving as reconnaissance for potential alien contact or the retrieval of extraterrestrial technology?

The lines between government and private ventures blurred during Obama's era, leading some to question whether private companies were being used as fronts for secretive government operations. While the Obama administration promoted its partnership with the private sector as a way to drive down the costs of space travel and encourage innovation, skeptics saw something more: a calculated move to obscure the true nature of deep-space missions under the guise of commercial interests. The strategic direction to hand over much of the low-Earth orbit responsibilities to private companies—while maintaining governmental control over more mysterious deep-space ventures—only fueled these suspicions.

John Podesta, a key figure in Obama's administration and a longtime advocate for UFO disclosure, further added to the intrigue. As Obama's senior advisor and co-director of his transition team, Podesta had made no secret of his desire to open up the government's UFO files. His famous remark from 2002 echoed throughout the disclosure community:

I think it's time to open the books on things that have remained in the dark; on the questions of government investigations of UFOs. It's time to find out what the truth really is that's out there. We ought to do it because it's right; we ought to do it because the American people quite frankly can handle the truth; and we ought to do it because it's the law.[64]

Yet, despite his position of influence, Podesta was unable to bring about the kind of transparency many had hoped for during Obama's two terms, admitting: "Finally, my biggest failure of 2014, once again not securing the disclosure of UFO files."[65]

This disconnect between Podesta's advocacy and the administration's silence on extraterrestrial matters left UFO enthusiasts wondering: What was Obama privy to, and why was disclosure kept off the table?

Though Obama himself made lighthearted comments about UFOs during his presidency, they did little to quell the belief that he knew more than he let on. In a 2021 late-night interview with television host James Corden, Obama said:

There is footage and records of objects in the skies. We don't know exactly what they are. We can't explain how they moved, their trajectory. They did not have an easily explainable pattern.[66]

His administration's strategic choices in space policy, combined with its reluctance to engage publicly with the UFO phenomenon in detail, have since left a lasting legacy of speculation. This silence has only deepened the mystery surrounding what the government may know about extraterrestrial life and the possible role that space exploration—whether through NASA or private enterprises—might play in uncovering or concealing these truths.

In 2011, the FBI launched "The Vault," an online repository of declassified documents, which included the notorious Hottel Memo—an FBI memo from 1950 discussing alleged flying saucers recovered in

New Mexico. While this document had been available for decades, its sudden resurfacing reignited public curiosity about UFOs, especially given the administration's simultaneous shift in space policy. Some viewed this as a breadcrumb trail, a signal from within the government that there was indeed something more to the UFO story than the official narrative suggested. Yet, Obama's administration remained tight-lipped, leaving the most burning questions unanswered.

As the Obama era came to a close, it became evident that while the president had not engaged directly with UFO disclosure, his impact on the future of space exploration was profound. By realigning NASA's focus and empowering private companies to lead the charge into space, Obama set the stage for a new chapter in space exploration. Whether these moves were purely pragmatic or laced with hidden agendas remains a topic of ongoing debate. What is clear is that Obama's presidency catalyzed a shift in how the US approaches space—in terms of exploration and in the murkier domain of classified missions and possible extraterrestrial engagement.

While the public may never know the full extent of what was discussed behind closed doors in the Obama White House, his presidency's enduring legacy is the privatization of space and the unanswered questions that remain about the deeper motives driving America's space agenda. Was it truly just about exploration and innovation, or was something far more mysterious at play?

Donald Trump (2017–2021): The Space Force President

Donald Trump's first presidency left an indelible mark on the landscape of space policy, and his creation of the US Space Force in 2019 signaled a bold new era. Officially billed as a military branch dedicated to protecting US assets in space, the Space Force marked the first significant restructuring of the US Armed Forces since 1947. But while its stated mission was to ensure American dominance in the final frontier, many believe something far more enigmatic was driving this unprecedented move. Was the Space Force, as the administration claimed, purely about defense, or could it have been created in response to classified knowledge involving extraterrestrial threats?

At first glance, the establishment of the Space Force seemed like a logical evolution in response to growing concerns over the militarization of space by foreign powers. Countries like China and Russia were making aggressive advancements in space technology, and the fear of satellite warfare was on the rise. However, speculation soon emerged that the real reason for the Space Force was more clandestine. Trump's cryptic public statements about space, alongside his administration's focus on secrecy around UFO-related matters, raised serious questions about whether the US government was preparing for a conflict that transcended geopolitical borders. Could the Space Force have been created not to protect against human adversaries, but against an extraterrestrial presence? In a 2020 NBC interview, Trump said to his son, Donald Trump Jr., and the world, "I won't talk to you about what I know about [Roswell], but it's very interesting…". [Asked by his son to declassify it, he said,] "Well, I'll have to think about that one."[67]

Haim Eshed, a highly credible and decorated individual in the realm of space security, only added fuel to the fire with his shocking revelations. Eshed, the former head of Israel's space security program and a respected figure in the international scientific community, had overseen satellite launches and space defense for nearly thirty years. His credentials were unquestionable. So when he claimed in late 2020 that extraterrestrial beings exist, and both the US and Israeli governments had been in contact with them for years, the world took notice.

Eshed went even further, stating that there exists a "Galactic Federation," a group of extraterrestrial entities that have communicated with global leaders. According to Eshed, Donald Trump was on the verge of revealing this information to the public during his presidency, but was reportedly persuaded not to by this extraterrestrial group. The reason given? Humanity, as Eshed claimed, "was not yet ready" for such a revelation.[68]

Trump's relationship with space policy wasn't limited to defense. His administration revived US interest in lunar exploration through the Artemis program, which aims to return humans to the moon and establish a permanent presence on its surface. While this seemed like a continuation of the Cold War space race, some began to wonder if there was more behind this sudden push for lunar exploration. The timing, coinciding with the formation of the Space Force, led conspiracy theorists to speculate that the US government was aware of something hidden on the moon—possibly an extraterrestrial artifact or base—and that Artemis was a cover for a more covert mission. Was the real objective of the Artemis program to uncover or defend something long kept secret by previous administrations?

Trump himself has been anything but subtle when it comes to making cryptic statements that fuel these suspicions. In a 2018 interview, he remarked, "Space is the world's newest warfighting domain. Amid grave threats to our national security, American superiority in space is absolutely vital." Though his remarks were ostensibly aimed at foreign powers, some observers wondered if Trump was referring to an entirely different kind of threat. Was he hinting at a cosmic conflict far beyond the understanding of the average citizen?

The Trump administration's handling of UFO-related issues only added fuel to the fire. Trump oversaw the unprecedented declassification of military footage depicting unidentified aerial phenomena. The Pentagon confirmed that these objects displayed capabilities far beyond known human technology. While this might have been seen as a step toward transparency, skeptics believe it was merely a distraction from much larger secrets still being withheld. If the government was now willing to acknowledge UAPs publicly, what classified information was still being concealed? Was the Space Force part of a secretive plan to prepare for extraterrestrial encounters?

Further deepening the mystery was Trump's fascination with military might and dominance in space. His administration was also notable for accelerating efforts to modernize America's nuclear arsenal—an unusual focus, considering that space-based defense systems, like those envisioned in the Strategic Defense Initiative during the Reagan years, had long fallen out of favor. Some conspiracy theorists posit that the simultaneous focus on nuclear modernization and space defense could indicate the administration's awareness of a looming extraterrestrial threat that necessitated both terrestrial and space-based military readiness. In a 2024 podcast interview, Trump both gave credence to and cast doubt on the subject of UFOs. He remarked:

> I have met with pilots…they are not conspiratorial, they are not crazy, and they tell me stories that they've seen things that you wouldn't believe. Am I a believer? No, I can't say I am. But I have met with people, serious people, that say there are some really strange things flying around out there.[69]

Trump's establishment of the Space Force also begs the question of why the initiative was launched so abruptly. If the US had been in space for decades and had overseen numerous space defense systems under previous administrations, why the sudden need for a new, independent branch of the military dedicated exclusively to space operations? One possible answer lies in the belief that Trump's administration received classified intelligence on the existence of hostile extraterrestrial entities or interdimensional threats, and that the Space Force was created as a precautionary measure against a threat the public would never fully understand.

Moreover, the push to establish a permanent US presence on the moon under the Artemis program has led to speculation that this move was less about exploration and more about militarization. Some UFO researchers suggest the moon has long been a point of interest for secret military operations, and classified reports from previous lunar missions indicate the discovery of unknown structures or artifacts. Could the Space Force's true mission be to secure and monitor these mysterious locations? The creation of the Space Force, combined with the moon initiative, seems almost too coincidental for those who believe in the existence of an extraterrestrial presence that governments around the world are attempting to monitor, manage, or control.

Adding yet another layer to this intrigue is the timing of Trump's decision to release the Pentagon's UFO files. While it was lauded by UFO enthusiasts as a step toward full disclosure, the fact that the information was released so close to the creation of the Space Force raises eyebrows. Was this just a calculated move to manage public perception, or could it have been part of a larger, slow-drip disclosure plan—preparing the public for the eventual revelation of something far more profound than we've been led to believe?

Ultimately, Donald Trump's first presidency and the creation of the Space Force have left the door wide open for speculation. Was the Space Force simply an extension of America's ongoing military dominance, or was it a reaction to classified knowledge far beyond the comprehension of the average citizen? Whether Trump was indeed privy to extraterrestrial secrets remains a mystery, but his cryptic comments and bold moves in space policy have ensured that the questions surrounding his role in space defense will linger for years to come.

Looking Ahead

As Lyndon B. Johnson's era drew to a close, America found itself at a crossroads—on one hand, poised to achieve unparalleled triumphs in space, and on the other, grappling with the shadowy undercurrent of UFO secrecy. Johnson's contributions to space exploration laid the groundwork for the Apollo moon landings under Nixon, but his silence on key UFO incidents, like Kecksburg and the Malmstrom ICBM shutdown, left lingering questions. What did he know? Or, more troublingly, what was he kept from knowing?

Johnson's legacy is one of contrast: He was celebrated for his space achievements, but forever tied to the growing web of UFO secrecy that would shape the presidencies to come. As the nation looks to the stars, it must also wonder: What hidden truths about the skies above were left in the shadows during Johnson's time, and who controls them now?

Richard Nixon would claim the moon, but his presidency would soon be entangled in the murky realities of UFOs and the secretive forces that continue to haunt the corridors of power.

Chapter 8

THE INSIDER PRESIDENT AND
THE GOVERNMENT'S UFO DOCUMENTARY

It is of great importance to set a resolution, not to be shaken, never to tell an untruth. There is no vice so mean, so pitiful, so contemptible; and he who permits himself to tell a lie once, finds it much easier to do it a second and a third time, till at length it becomes habitual; he tells lies without attending to it, and truths without the world's believing him. This falsehood of the tongue leads to that of the heart, and in time depraves all its good disposition.

—THOMAS JEFFERSON

Richard Nixon and UFOs:
The President Who Came Closest to Disclosure

Richard Nixon's presidency was a unique turning point in American history, not just because of the monumental scandals or his foreign policy successes, but for his relationship with UFO secrets. Nixon, unlike his predecessors John F. Kennedy and Lyndon B. Johnson, had insider knowledge of classified information on UFOs from his years serving as vice president under Dwight D. Eisenhower. His time in the Eisenhower administration gave him access to many military and intelligence secrets, including the controversial subject of unidentified aerial phenomena.

Nixon's UFO involvement becomes even more compelling when considering his connections to two pivotal figures in the realm of potential disclosure—writer Robert Emenegger and producer Allan Sandler. These men created the NBC documentary *UFOs: Past, Present and Future* in the early 1970s, which revealed government handling of the UFO phenomenon in an unprecedented way. Though few know it, this project had the quiet backing of the Nixon administration. However, Watergate would soon derail any hope of UFO transparency.

Nixon's Early Engagement with UFOs

Nixon's familiarity with UFO-related secrets likely began in the 1950s under Eisenhower, who took the issue seriously. Eisenhower's administration reportedly held meetings about UFO incidents, and Nixon, as vice president, was present for many of these discussions. This meant Nixon already knew what the public did not—there were documented instances of UAPs that military officials couldn't easily explain. While the US Air Force, through projects like Blue Book, publicly dismissed the significance of UFO sightings, Nixon remained an insider to the real discussions happening behind closed doors.

Though Nixon's early years were marked by political and electoral defeats, his 1968 presidential victory brought him back to the seat of power, and with it, the ability to influence how the government handled UFOs. His longtime friendship with Jackie Gleason, a comedian who had a deep obsession with UFOs, only stoked the flames of Nixon's interest in the extraterrestrial question. Gleason, whose home was famously shaped like a flying saucer, was far more than a casual believer in UFOs; he was a serious researcher. This friendship would later lead to one of the most tantalizing and controversial stories of UFO lore.

The Jackie Gleason Incident: Nixon's Secret Trip to Homestead AFB

One of the most provocative pieces of Nixon's UFO history comes from his connection to Gleason and the alleged incident at Homestead Air Force Base (AFB). In 1974, Beverly McKittrick, Gleason's ex-wife, claimed that Nixon took Gleason on a late-night trip to the base, where they were shown the remains of extraterrestrial beings recovered from a crashed UFO. According to McKittrick, this incident left Gleason visibly shaken for weeks.

Though Gleason never publicly confirmed the story, he didn't deny it, either. The legend surrounding the visit to Homestead AFB only grew, with variations suggesting Nixon personally escorted Gleason or Gleason was taken to see the bodies by military personnel at Nixon's request. While many historians and UFO skeptics dismiss this story as improbable, given the high security surrounding presidents, the narrative has endured, fueled by McKittrick's consistent retelling of events.

What's clear from this episode is Nixon's willingness to engage with the UFO issue behind the scenes. His close friendship with Gleason gave him an outlet to explore the phenomenon more freely than perhaps any president before or after him.

UFO Documentary: Nixon's Quiet Disclosure Effort

In addition to the Homestead AFB incident, Nixon's interest in UFOs materialized in more official capacities. By the early 1970s, the US government was subtly warming to the idea of public disclosure—through the unlikely medium of a documentary. Robert Emenegger and Allan Sandler, under the quiet participation of the Department of Defense, produced *UFOs: Past, Present and Future*, a landmark documentary that proposed the possibility of extraterrestrial life and government encounters with UFOs.

The Nixon administration played a significant role in allowing Emenegger and Sandler access to sensitive military footage and interviews. While the final cut of the documentary didn't include explosive revelations, many UFO researchers believe it was intended to be part of

Nixon's broader disclosure strategy—one that would slowly introduce the public to the reality of UFOs. However, the timing couldn't have been worse.

As *UFOs: Past, Present and Future* was being finalized, the Watergate scandal erupted, engulfing Nixon's presidency in controversy. The president, once riding high on a historic reelection landslide, saw his power diminish overnight. His influence over UFO-related initiatives dissipated, and the documentary, once positioned as a bold step toward disclosure, was relegated to a mere curiosity.

Watergate: The End of Nixon's UFO Disclosure

Watergate wasn't just the end of Nixon's presidency; it was the end of his pursuit of UFO transparency. The same Nixon who had opened China to the world and negotiated arms limitations with the Soviet Union had once envisioned a groundbreaking disclosure of extraterrestrial life—a revelation that would have placed him in the annals of history as one of the most transformative presidents. Yet, the fallout from Watergate dashed any hope of further progress.

While *UFOs: Past, Present and Future* remains a critical piece of UFO history, it is also a symbol of missed opportunity. Nixon had the power, connections, and willingness to move the UFO narrative forward, but fate—and scandal—intervened. His administration stands as the closest any president has come to pulling back the veil on the extraterrestrial enigma.

Looking Ahead

As we contemplate the untapped potential of Nixon's legacy in UFO history, the lingering question remains: What cosmic secrets slipped through the cracks of his administration's untimely downfall? Nixon's knowledge and relationships hinted at something far more profound—truths that may never have seen the light of day. But his exit didn't close the door on governmental engagement with the UFO enigma.

With the arrival of Gerald Ford, a new chapter in UFO disclosure dawned—one marked by public demands for answers. Unlike Nixon's more veiled approach, Ford openly challenged the government's silence. His push for public investigations threw the UFO debate into the political spotlight. Yet, despite his best efforts, secrecy continued to reign. Ford's administration, shaped by influential figures like Donald Rumsfeld and Dick Cheney, walked a precarious line between transparency and protecting classified truths.

This era also gave rise to one of the most infamous controversies: the "swamp gas" explanation. Instead of quelling public curiosity, it ignited a firestorm of speculation, deepening the mystery and skepticism surrounding UFO phenomena.

In the next chapter, we delve deeper into Ford's bold inquiry, exploring how his administration's push for transparency collided with forces bent on keeping certain answers forever hidden. As Project Blue Book takes center stage, the struggle between exposing the truth and maintaining the veil of secrecy intensifies. What was truly at stake, and who stood to lose the most if the full story came to light?

Chapter 9

THE PIVOT PRESIDENT
AND PROJECT BLUE BOOK

> The essence of Government is power; and power, lodged as
> it must be in human hands, will ever be liable to abuse.
>
> —JAMES MADISON

The Ford Inquiry:
UFOs, Government, and a Nation on Edge

In the spring of 1966, the American public found itself captivated by strange lights in the sky. Reports of UFOs were nothing new, but something about the Michigan sightings that year stirred the pot more than usual. The small town of Dexter in that state became the focal point of what was, for a time, one of the most publicized UFO waves in US history. Sightings occurred night after night, and were often witnessed by dozens of people—including police officers, who could hardly be considered unreliable witnesses.

As the number of reports escalated, the US Air Force dispatched Dr. J. Allen Hynek, their consultant and an astrophysicist, to investigate. When Hynek arrived in Michigan, expectations were high. Would the Air Force finally admit to something extraordinary? Or would the curtain of official secrecy remain drawn tight? The country would soon have its answer—and it wasn't what the public wanted to hear.

In a hastily arranged press conference, Hynek delivered his verdict: The strange lights in Dexter's sky were nothing more than "swamp gas," a natural occurrence caused by the decay of organic material in marshy areas. The explanation was met with widespread ridicule and disbelief. For many, it felt like the government was once again dismissing their experiences, as though the public was too naïve or too ignorant to handle the truth.

One man, however, wasn't willing to let the story fade quietly into the night: Congressman Gerald R. Ford. As the House minority leader and a representative from Michigan, Ford had received a flood of letters and telegrams demanding answers. The congressman, a person of methodical and serious temperament, knew this wasn't just a passing phase of American curiosity. He believed something more was at play—and the people deserved to know what.

Thus, Ford began to push for a congressional investigation into UFOs, a proposal that would later become a historical footnote in his career, and one of the few moments when UFOs would briefly step into the political limelight.

The Ford Push for Transparency

Ford's move was both surprising and timely. UFOs had long been the subject of speculation and conspiracy, but rarely had such calls for transparency come from such a high political office. In a letter dated March 28, 1966, Ford addressed two powerful congressional chairmen: Rep. George P. Miller of the Science and Astronautics Committee and Rep. L. Mendel Rivers of the Armed Services Committee. Ford's message was clear—he wanted public hearings on the UFO phenomenon. He believed the Air Force's dismissive explanations weren't enough. Challenging the official narrative, Ford wrote:

No doubt you have noted the recent flurry of newspaper stories about unidentified flying objects (UFOs). I have taken special interest in these accounts because many of the latest reported sightings have been in my home state of Michigan.... I do not agree that all of these reports can be or should be so easily explained away.[70]

He continued, calling for testimony from the executive branch and civilians who had claimed to witness these objects. His tone was measured but firm:

The American people are entitled to a more thorough explanation than has been given them by the Air Force to date.... The time has come for the President or Congress to name an objective and respected panel to investigate, appraise, and report on all present and future evidence about what is going on.[71]

This wasn't the voice of a man who subscribed to wild conspiracy theories. Ford was pragmatic, even skeptical, by nature. But he was also keenly aware of the growing disconnect between what the government was saying and what the people believed. For Ford, it wasn't just about UFOs; it was about the erosion of trust between the public and its leaders.

The Swamp Gas Incident: A Public Relations Disaster

The "swamp gas" explanation may have been the spark that ignited Ford's push for an investigation, but it was far from the only fuel. The Michigan UFO flap was just the latest in a series of sightings stretching back decades. Project Blue Book, the Air Force's official investigation into UFOs, had been running since 1952, but by 1966, its credibility was in shambles.

Behind the scenes, many officials were becoming increasingly frustrated with the public's clamor for answers. UFO reports were flooding in, and while many could be easily explained away, some defied conventional explanation. Yet, for every serious investigation, there were twice as many dismissals, fueling the sense that the government was hiding something.

When Dr. Hynek stood before the press and attributed the sightings to swamp gas, it was a calculated move, but it backfired spectacularly. Public opinion turned swiftly. How could dozens of witnesses, including seasoned police officers, all have mistaken swamp gas for something more otherworldly?

Ford seized on this moment of doubt. He wasn't proclaiming that little green men were visiting Earth, but he understood that the Air Force's lackluster explanations weren't quelling public curiosity. Instead, they were feeding conspiracy. The more the government tried to brush off the reports, the more people believed there was something to hide.

The Congressional Fight for Answers

Ford's insistence on a congressional inquiry wasn't just about UFOs; it was about setting a precedent. He believed in the integrity of public service and the importance of transparency in government. In the face of growing distrust, he called for an open and honest investigation. This, after all, was an era of Cold War paranoia, when anything unexplained was immediately seen as a potential threat.

Yet, despite Ford's efforts, the push for public hearings faced resistance. Powerful figures in Congress were hesitant to engage in discussions about the subject, fearing it would open a Pandora's box of public hysteria. Additionally, the Air Force, long the gatekeepers of UFO information, seemed uninterested in providing more than the bare minimum.

Ford's proposed hearings never materialized in the form he had envisioned. Instead, the Air Force promised a new study—this one supposedly free from military influence. They selected the University of Colorado to conduct an independent investigation, led by physicist Dr. Edward Condon. Known as the Condon Committee, this would later become one of the most infamous chapters in the history of UFO investigations.

The Legacy of the Condon Committee

While Ford's push for transparency may not have resulted in immediate congressional action, it did spark the formation of the Condon Committee. For Ford, this was at least a step in the right direction. The committee was meant to be an independent scientific inquiry, free from the biases of the Air Force or other governmental agencies.

However, as history would show, the Condon Committee's findings would once again leave the public divided. The group ultimately concluded that there was no evidence of extraterrestrial visitors and UFOs posed no threat to national security. But for many, the committee's findings were just another carefully orchestrated dismissal.

Despite the outcome, Ford's efforts weren't in vain. He had forced the UFO matter into the halls of Congress and into the public discourse. His push for accountability in government resonated far beyond the 1966 Michigan sightings. In an era marked by secrecy, from the Cold War to Vietnam, Ford's insistence on transparency, even in the face of ridicule, was a rare moment of political courage.

The Thin Line Between Fact and Conspiracy

The story of Gerald Ford's involvement in the UFO debate is a fascinating look at the intersection of government, public trust, and mystery. While Ford never explicitly stated that he believed in extraterrestrials, his push for an investigation raised the stakes. In doing so, he walked a fine line between political responsibility and the murky waters of conspiracy.

For decades, the subject of UFOs had occupied a strange place in American culture—caught somewhere between science fiction and plausible reality. For every witness who swore they had seen something inexplicable, there was a skeptic armed with a perfectly rational explanation. Yet Ford understood that the truth, whatever it might be, needed to be explored openly. The public's belief that something was being hidden was as dangerous as the phenomena themselves.

Ford's inquiry, and the resulting Condon Committee, may not have provided the definitive answers the public sought, but it was a critical moment in the ongoing debate. The American government had been forced to address the UFO mystery head-on—and, for a brief moment, the door to transparency had been cracked open.

As Ford's career would later ascend to the presidency, the UFO question would remain unresolved—an open case file in the annals of American history. But in 1966, the man who would one day occupy the Oval Office made it clear: The American people deserved the truth, no matter how unsettling it might be.

UFOs in the Ford Administration: Secrets at the Highest Level

When Gerald Ford assumed the presidency following the resignation of Richard Nixon, Ford's administration seemed poised to continue the status quo of governance. Yet, beneath the surface of the Ford White House, something more mysterious and possibly significant was taking place—an ongoing interest in unidentified flying objects and extraterrestrial phenomena.

At the heart of this enigma was Donald Rumsfeld, Ford's close confidant and a man of immense political influence. Ford had known Rumsfeld since their days in Congress, and when Ford became president, he appointed Rumsfeld first as his chief of staff and later as secretary of defense. During these years, Rumsfeld appeared to have a curious but deep interest in UFOs—a curiosity that has led many to wonder what the true role of the Ford administration was in dealing with these mysterious aerial events.

Two letters, now housed in the Ford Presidential Library, provide a tantalizing glimpse into the White House's interest in UFOs. The first was written on March 3, 1975, by Dr. J. Allen Hynek (who had attributed the Michigan sightings to "swamp gas"), then director of the

Center for UFO Studies, to Donald Rumsfeld. In the letter, Hynek, at Rumsfeld's request, provided updates on the latest developments within the Center. The second, Rumsfeld's brief but intriguing reply, came just days later, on March 12, 1975. In his response, Rumsfeld thanked Hynek for the material and referred to the UFO topic as a "phenomenon"—a word choice that raised more questions than it answered.

The Correspondence That Sparked Questions

At first glance, this exchange might seem trivial—an example of Rumsfeld maintaining professional courtesy with a respected scientist. However, for those familiar with UFO history, the implications are far more significant. Rumsfeld's use of the word "phenomenon" is particularly revealing. According to the Merriam-Webster Dictionary, "phenomenon" refers to "an observable fact or event." Rumsfeld could have used any number of terms to describe the UFO material—for example, "theories," "anomalies," or "claims"—but he chose a word that suggests a certain level of acceptance of, if not belief in, the reality of these unexplained sightings.

What did Rumsfeld know? Why was the secretary of defense, a man tasked with overseeing the nation's most advanced military technologies, corresponding with one of the leading UFO researchers of the time? Some speculate that Rumsfeld, far from being a passive observer, was keeping a close eye on UFO developments. Was this at the behest of his boss, President Ford, who had previously called for government transparency on UFOs? Or was Rumsfeld acting on his own, driven by a more personal curiosity about extraterrestrial phenomena?

Rumsfeld, Cheney, and UFOs: A Hidden Agenda?

Rumsfeld wasn't the only powerful figure in the Ford administration linked to UFO issues. Dick Cheney, a close friend of Rumsfeld, was also rising in prominence during this time. After Rumsfeld' appointment as secretary of defense, Cheney was tapped to become Ford's chief of staff. These two men, who would go on to become key players in US defense and intelligence policy for decades to come, were deeply connected, both professionally and, as some believe, through a shared interest in the extraterrestrial.

UFO researchers have long speculated that Rumsfeld and Cheney had insider knowledge about the government's involvement with UFO phenomena, stretching back to their early days in power.[72] As close confidants in the White House, did they coordinate efforts to track civilian UFO research? Was Hynek's Center for UFO Studies, a widely respected organization, being monitored by these high-level government officials to ensure that no sensitive information would be leaked to the public?

The idea that Cheney and Rumsfeld were part of a larger cover-up of UFO intelligence isn't new, but the letters between Rumsfeld and Hynek add new weight to these suspicions. Why would the secretary of defense be interested in updates from a civilian UFO study group? What information did Hynek have that Rumsfeld felt was worth tracking? The secrecy surrounding their communications leaves much to be imagined.

UFOs as a National Security Concern

In the 1970s, the world was in the grip of Cold War tensions. As the United States vied for technological and military supremacy against the Soviet Union, the idea of unidentified objects flying in US airspace became a matter of national security. Could some UFO sightings have been advanced Soviet technology? Or, even more concerning, was there a threat from beyond Earth that needed to be kept from public knowledge to prevent widespread panic?

Rumsfeld's role as secretary of defense placed him in a unique position. Not only did he have access to the highest levels of classified military information, but he was also responsible for safeguarding the nation from any potential threats. If UFOs posed a genuine risk—whether from an adversarial nation or an extraterrestrial source—it would make sense that Rumsfeld would want to stay informed. This brings us back to his communications with Hynek: Were they merely updates out of curiosity, or was Rumsfeld part of a broader initiative to control the flow of UFO-related information to and from civilian researchers?

The Ford Silence: Was He Briefed into Secrecy?

It's striking that after becoming president, Ford, a man who once vocally advocated for a congressional investigation into UFOs, suddenly became silent on the issue. What happened between Ford's days in Congress and his time in the White House that changed his stance? One theory is that Ford was briefed—perhaps by Rumsfeld or Cheney—on classified information regarding UFOs. Armed with this new knowledge, Ford may have decided the truth was too dangerous to share with the public.

The UFO community has long speculated that many US presidents, once in office, are informed on the existence of extraterrestrial phenomena, but are discouraged from pursuing the issue publicly. Could Ford have been one of these presidents, brought into the fold of secrecy and asked to keep quiet? If so, Rumsfeld and Cheney, key figures in his administration, would have been integral in managing this sensitive information.

While we may never know the full extent of Rumsfeld's and Cheney's involvement in UFO matters, the evidence we do have points to a consistent pattern of interest and control. From their early days in the Ford administration to their later roles in shaping US defense and intelligence policies, these men have always been at the center of the nation's most secretive affairs. The question that remains is how much of that secrecy involved knowledge of extraterrestrial phenomena.

Secrets That Endure

The letters between Rumsfeld and Hynek, though brief, provide a window into the Ford administration's interest in UFO phenomena. The involvement of Rumsfeld and Cheney, two of the most powerful figures in American politics at the time, raises significant questions about what the government knew—and still knows—about UFOs. Was Ford, like other presidents before him, sworn to secrecy after taking office? And were Rumsfeld and Cheney the gatekeepers of that secret, ensuring that the truth about UFOs remained hidden from public view?

As we look back on these events, one thing is clear: The Ford administration's engagement with UFO issues wasn't as superficial as it may have seemed. The intrigue continues, and the truth, as always, remains just out of reach.

Looking Ahead

Government secrets don't just challenge political power; they confront the very foundations of faith. The Founding Fathers, many of whom were deeply influenced by Christian beliefs, built this nation on principles drawn from their understanding of the Creator and His order in the cosmos. Yet, the possibility of intelligent life beyond Earth raises profound theological questions. Could these beings fit into the Creator's grand design? Or would their existence challenge the very beliefs that shaped the birth of America? These aren't just speculative questions; they touch the core of who we are as a people and what we believe about God, the universe, and our place in it.

But the mystery extends far beyond government halls and political maneuvering. As we step into the next chapter, we will grapple with a question even more profound: How does the existence of extraterrestrial life intersect with the deepest truths of human faith? Could these cosmic revelations disrupt the very foundation of biblical theology, or do the Scriptures themselves hold the keys to understanding the universe's greatest mysteries? Join me as we unravel the tension between what we know, what we believe, and the staggering possibilities that lie just beyond the stars.

Chapter 10

THE CREATOR'S UNIVERSE: BIBLICAL THEOLOGY AND THE TENSION OF EXTRATERRESTRIAL LIFE

> We hold these truths to be self-evident, that all men are created equal; that they are endowed by their Creator with inherent and unalienable rights.
>
> —The Declaration of Independence

As we've seen in the previous chapters, history has recorded significant moments when government officials and presidents have wrestled with the reality of UFOs and the possibility of extraterrestrial life. These accounts raise questions that extend beyond national security and public policy. They touch on fundamental issues of human existence, creation, and the nature of the universe—questions that cannot be answered by politics or science alone.

While the historical responses have shaped public understanding, there remains a deeper, more profound layer to this conversation. The mysteries surrounding extraterrestrial encounters not only challenge our understanding of the physical world, but also demand that we explore the spiritual dimensions of these phenomena. What do these encounters mean for humanity's relationship with the divine? How do they fit within the biblical framework of a supernatural cosmos?

As we now turn to the theological perspective, we will explore how Scripture and Christian doctrine address the possibility of otherworldly beings, the reality of spiritual warfare, and the role of divine intervention in these events. By shifting from the political to the theological, we seek to understand how the eternal truths of the Bible offer insight into these modern realities.

The Creator and His Expansive Cosmos

As scientific discovery advances, theologians are increasingly confronted with an ancient, yet ever more relevant, question: Could God, the Creator of all things, have made intelligent life on other planets? Some ancient theologians believed so. Saint John Henry Newman (AD 1801–1890), an English theologian, wrote:

> In the controversy about the Plurality of worlds, it has been considered…to be so necessary that the Creator should have filled with living beings the luminaries which we see in the sky, and the other cosmical bodies which we imagine there, that it almost amounts to a blasphemy to doubt it.[73]

Hans Küng, University of Tübingen (Germany) theologian, asserts that "we must allow for living beings, intelligent—although quite different—living beings, also on other stars of the immense universe."[74]

Similarly, University of Notre Dame scholar Thomas O'Meara speculates with eager anticipation, suggesting that "there might be a number of modes of supernatural life with God, a variety of God's more intimate life shared with intelligent creatures in a billion galaxies."[75]

The vastness of the universe challenges the traditional notion of humanity as the sole focus of God's redemptive plan. Some have suggested that the biblical term *kosmos* (John 3:16) means that God's care and love might extend far beyond Earth, encompassing all galaxies, stars, and possible life forms scattered throughout the cosmos. Can

God's promise of transformation, achieved through the resurrection of Jesus Christ, apply to life beyond our planet? This chapter explores that possibility and the theological implications for humanity and potential extraterrestrial beings by examining various biblical texts, Jewish mystical traditions, medieval philosophy, and modern theological speculation.

As we consider the vastness of the universe, we must return to the core of Christian theology: humanity's place in creation. The Bible offers a unique perspective on this, presenting humanity as the bearer of the *imago Dei*. But could this divine image extend beyond Earth, potentially to intelligent beings on other planets? Let's dive deeper into the implications of this possibility.

The Creation of the Cosmos and the Imago Dei

The Bible starts with a story that describes humanity as being made in the "image of God," or *imago Dei* (Genesis 1:26–27). This idea has traditionally meant that humans have a special relationship with God and are given the responsibility to care for creation.

However, if intelligent beings exist on other planets, would they also share in the *imago Dei*? The Bible is silent on extraterrestrial life, yet early Jewish texts and mystical traditions seem open to the idea of a populated cosmos. Rabbi Hasdai Crescas (1340–1410 CE), in his philosophical work, *Light of the Lord*, was among the first to propose that space is infinite and contains a potentially infinite number of worlds.[76] Crescas argued that nothing in Scripture or Talmudic writings denies the existence of extraterrestrial life. In fact, in postulating what God does at night, he cites the Talmud, which hints at the multiplicity of worlds when it describes God traversing "eighteen thousand worlds on his chariot" (Talmud Avoda Zara 3b).[77]

In Jewish mystical tradition, the Zohar adds another layer of complexity by suggesting that the righteous, or *tzaddikim*, will rule over their own worlds. Rabbi Pinchas Eliyahu Horowitz of Vilna (1765–1821 CE) expanded on this, suggesting these eighteen thousand worlds are inhabited by intelligent life forms that God wishes to visit periodically.[78] This raises a key theological question: Could the *imago Dei* extend beyond Earth, encompassing extraterrestrial beings who, like humans, are capable of relating to God and participating in His divine purposes?

If the *imago Dei* opens the door for intelligent life beyond Earth, another question quickly follows: Would these beings share in humanity's fall, or are they untouched by sin? The Bible's silence on extraterrestrial life leaves us with many possibilities, and both Christian and Jewish traditions provide intriguing hints. Could sin be a local, earthbound event, or does its impact ripple across the entire cosmos? The answer may reshape our understanding of divine redemption.

The Fall and Sin: Local or Universal?

Christian theology traditionally teaches that Adam and Eve's fall into sin affected all of creation (Genesis 3; Romans 8:22). But if intelligent beings exist on other planets, are they also subject to the corruption brought about by humanity's fall, or is the fall a localized, earthbound event?

Catholic Dominican philosopher Tommaso Campanella (1568–1639), OP,[79] in his *Apologia pro Galileo* (1622), defended Galileo by taking a different stance: Christ did not need to be crucified multiple times for the beings on each star, just as He did not need to be crucified again for the inhabitants of the Antipodes, who hadn't heard of Him. Even if extraterrestrials were of the same species as humans, Campanella argued, they wouldn't have been affected by Adam's original sin, and therefore would not require redemption unless they had committed some other sin.[80]

Rabbi Crescas' earlier work also left room for the idea that extraterrestrial beings might exist in a different state from humanity. In his understanding, God's engagement with eighteen thousand worlds could mean each world has its own relationship with the Creator, independent of humanity's fall. This view aligns with later Kabbalistic thought, which suggests God's righteous servants govern various worlds, perhaps indicating that some of these worlds may not have experienced a fall at all.

If extraterrestrial beings exist without the stain of original sin, their relationship with God would differ from that of humanity, leading to profound theological questions about the nature of redemption and grace.

But what about the heart of Christian theology—the incarnation of Christ? If intelligent life exists elsewhere, does Christ's redemptive work on Earth extend to them as well? Or would God need to take on flesh in each world, adapting salvation to each species? These questions have fascinated theologians for centuries, and their answers could challenge long-held doctrines about the nature of salvation.

The Incarnation: One Christ for All or Many Incarnations?

One of the central challenges to Christian theology posed by the possibility of extraterrestrial life concerns the incarnation of Christ. Would the *Logos*, the divine Word, need to take on flesh in multiple worlds to save different species, or is Christ's one-time incarnation on Earth sufficient for all? Some theologians argue that Christ's single act of redemption could extend to all of creation, including intelligent life forms across the cosmos, while others suggest each species might require its own salvific event.

Medieval Catholic philosopher William Vorilong (1392–1463) speculated that Christ's death on Earth could indeed redeem inhabitants of other worlds. He argued that Christ's singular sacrifice might extend to the entire cosmos, implying a universal scope for His redemptive work:[81]

> If it be inquired whether men exist on that world, and whether they have sinned as Adam sinned, I answer no, for they would not exist in sin and did not spring from Adam.... As to the question whether Christ by dying on this earth could redeem the inhabitants of another world, I answer that he is able to do this even if the worlds were infinite, but it would not be fitting for him to go unto another world that he must die again.[82]

Similarly, Scottish theologian Frederick Cronholm rejected the notion that Jesus would need to embark on successive missions of salvation from planet to planet to redeem every fallen species. In his reflection, he wrote, "'Is there a Bethlehem in Venus, a Gethsemane in Jupiter, a Calvary in Saturn?' suggesting that each intelligent species might require its own salvific event."[83]

Yves Congar (1904–1995), a twentieth-century Catholic theologian, supported the idea that Christian doctrine leaves open the possibility of inhabited worlds, but acknowledged the difficulty in addressing how Christ's incarnation might apply to extraterrestrial life.

He writes:

As for the question whether, if these beings exist, they also would have been called by God to the life of grace and a supernatural revelation, no other answer can be given than this: "It is possible." Why not? But we know nothing whatever about it: it belongs to the realm of God's inviolable and sovereign freedom.

Could there have been an Incarnation in one of these inhabited worlds? Could the Word of God have taken flesh there and become a Martian, for instance, as we know that he became a man of this earth in Jesus Christ, brother of us sinful children of Adam? Or could the Father have been incarnated there, or the Holy Spirit?

St Paul tells us that we must be "wise unto sobriety", and this is the moment to remember it, for we are beginning to ask questions that encroach on a sphere which God reserves to himself.[84]

Theologians have been debating this issue for more than a thousand years, and more recently, it has gained traction with the emergence of exotheology[85] and astrotheology.[86] Some argue that the incarnation has a universal significance, suggesting Christ's single act of redemption extends to all of creation, including any intelligent life forms across the cosmos. Others, however, propose a different view, positing that Christ may have died on each planet for the redemption of each species individually. In the words of Gerhard DeVries (AD 1648–1705):

There are indeed many and weighty authors who stand in the battle line for the lunar inhabitants. Nevertheless, victory is certainly ours, for they are not easily armed by faith or reason.[87]

Ultimately, this ongoing debate highlights the complexities of reconciling theological doctrine with the vast possibilities of a universe that may be teeming with life, leaving many questions open to faith and interpretation.

The debate about Christ's incarnation brings us to an even broader question: the scope of redemption itself. Could the saving work of Christ extend universally, or would different species require their own path to God? As we explore the vast theological landscape of salvation, we find that the answer may not be as straightforward as we think.

Redemption and the Scope of Salvation: Universal or Species-Specific?

Redemption is central to Christian theology. Through Christ's death and resurrection, humanity is reconciled with God. This raises the question: If extraterrestrial life exists, would Christ's redemptive act also extend to these beings?

Saint Athanasius affirmed the cosmic scope of Christ's work, declaring, "For the presence of the Savior in the flesh was the price of death and the saving of the whole creation."[88] This implies that Christ's redemptive act might extend beyond humanity to encompass all of creation, including potential extraterrestrial life.

However, some theologians, like Hans Küng, have suggested that extraterrestrial beings might exist in a sinless state and thus wouldn't require the same type of redemption as humanity. If these beings have not fallen, their relationship with God could be one of continued righteousness rather than one of reconciliation.

The Jewish mystical tradition offers another perspective. The Zohar suggests that righteous individuals will rule over their own worlds, implying that some extraterrestrial beings may already live in a state of righteousness, possibly beyond the need for redemption.

Karl Barth emphasized the universality of Christ's atonement, proposing that His one-time act of salvation could suffice for all creation. C. S. Lewis, the renowned Christian apologist and author, delved into the concept of extraterrestrial life in his science fiction trilogy: *Out of the Silent Planet*, *Perelandra*, and *That Hideous Strength*. In these works, Lewis envisioned a universe populated by diverse intelligent beings, each having a unique relationship with God. Through this imaginative lens, Lewis explored the theological implications of life beyond Earth, offering creative reflections on how divine truths might unfold across different worlds.

In *Out of the Silent Planet*, Lewis presents a world (Malacandra) where the inhabitants have not experienced a fall into sin, unlike Earth. This suggests extraterrestrial beings might exist in a state of original innocence, not needing redemption in the way humanity does. Meanwhile, in *Perelandra*, Lewis explores a world on the brink of its own potential fall, but through divine intervention, that fall is prevented, raising the question of whether Christ's incarnation and redemptive act on Earth might be sufficient to extend to other worlds.

Throughout the trilogy, Lewis hints at the vastness of God's creation, where different species may have their own distinct relationships with the Creator. However, all intelligent beings remain subject to God's sovereignty, and divine truths apply universally, even if manifested in unique ways across the cosmos. Lewis also delves into the idea of cosmic spiritual warfare, portraying malevolent forces similar to Satan attempting to corrupt other worlds, emphasizing that the struggle between good and evil isn't limited to Earth alone.

In the end, Lewis leaves open the question of whether Christ's sacrifice is sufficient for all intelligent beings or if different forms of redemption are necessary for other species. His works invite readers to consider the theological implications of life beyond Earth without offering definitive answers, allowing for creative speculation on how God's plan for salvation might unfold across the universe.

Ultimately, this ongoing debate underscores the complexities of reconciling theological doctrine with the vast possibilities of a universe that

may be filled with life, leaving many questions open to faith and interpretation. The central question remains: Does Christ's redemptive work
extend universally to all intelligent beings, or would different forms of
salvation be required for other species? While Christian theology presents a range of perspectives, the possibility of extraterrestrial life invites
continued reflection on the scope of God's redemptive plan, encouraging theologians and believers alike to contemplate just how far Christ's
saving grace might reach.

As we ponder these profound theological questions, it's worth turning to an often-overlooked biblical narrative. The story of Meroz in the
book of Judges contains intriguing hints that have led some to wonder: Could extraterrestrial beings have played a role in the biblical past?
Though speculative, these interpretations invite us to look at familiar
Scriptures in a new light.

Meroz: A Biblical Reference to Extraterrestrial Life?

The biblical narrative contains a curious and often overlooked reference
that some suggest points to the existence of extraterrestrial beings. In
the Song of Deborah, found in Judges 5, the prophetess calls down a
curse on a place called Meroz for failing to come to the aid of the Lord
in battle. Note:

> **From the sky the stars fought. From their courses, they fought
> against Sisera.** The river Kishon swept them away, that ancient
> river, the river Kishon. My soul, march on with strength. Then the
> horse hoofs stamped because of the prancing, the prancing of their
> strong ones. "Curse **Meroz**," said Yahweh's angel. "**Curse bitterly
> its inhabitants, because they didn't come to help Yahweh, to help
> Yahweh against the mighty.**" (Judges 5:20–23, WEB)[89]

While some commentators suggest Meroz was a human settlement,
others have speculated it refers to a star or planetary system inhabited by

intelligent beings. Talmudic sources, such as *Mo'ed Katan 16a*, explore this ambiguity, noting that "some say that Meroz was [the name of] a great personage; others say that it was [the name of] a star, as it is written [there]: They fought from Heaven, the stars in their courses fought against Sisera."[90]

If Meroz was indeed a star, then this passage could imply that extraterrestrial beings from Meroz had free will, as they chose not to assist God in the battle against Sisera. This raises the question of whether intelligent life from other celestial bodies (assuming they exist) was expected to participate in divine activities, indicating a shared moral responsibility in the cosmic order.

To clarify the distinction between the angelic and extraterrestrial interpretations of this passage, it's important to examine the symbolic use of "stars" in Scripture. In many biblical contexts, stars are associated with divine beings or angels, particularly in Job 38:7, where the "morning stars" are described as singing together at the creation of the world, and Revelation 1:20, where stars represent angels. Thus, the stars "fighting" in Judges 5:20 could be understood as referring to angels acting under God's command in the battle against Sisera.

If the stars are interpreted as angels, then the curse on Meroz could be seen as directed against a *human city* (not a distant planet) that failed to act in alignment with God's divine will. This interpretation lines up with the traditional understanding of the passage as one of spiritual and moral failure by a human community.

On the other hand, the more speculative extraterrestrial interpretation views Meroz as a celestial body (not a human city) inhabited by intelligent life, suggesting that these beings chose not to intervene in the battle. This perspective opens the possibility that extraterrestrial life forms, much like angels, could have a role in God's cosmic plan, potentially exercising free will in their decisions to engage in or abstain from human affairs. This interpretation, while fantastical, remains totally speculative and hinges on an unnatural reading of the text.

Ultimately, while the extraterrestrial hypothesis adds a layer of intrigue, it isn't grounded in biblical symbolism and theological tradition. However, the controversial text invites readers to ponder the broader scope of God's creation and the possible involvement of otherworldly beings.

Eschatology and the New Creation: A Cosmic Renewal?

The Bible speaks of a future transformation of the cosmos in the eschaton, when God will create a New Heaven and a New Earth (Revelation 21:1). As we contemplate a New Heaven and a New Earth, the idea that other worlds might share in this redemption adds another layer to the eschatological promise. Could God's transformative power extend beyond Earth, renewing the entire universe?

Paul Davies and other some modern theologians say yes.

They speculate that the eschaton could encompass all intelligent life, transforming not just Earth but the entire universe. This aligns with the Kabbalistic view that God traverses eighteen thousand worlds, suggesting that each of these worlds might participate in the final fulfillment of God's redemptive plan.

Moritz claims this eschatological renewal includes both continuity and discontinuity: Some elements of the present creation will carry forward, while others will be radically transformed. Science may help reveal some of the mysteries that point to the New Creation.

Throughout this chapter, we've examined the theological implications of life beyond Earth, tackling intricate questions about the incarnation, the fall, and the vast scope of salvation. But as we ponder the possibility of extraterrestrial life, another thought emerges: What if the visitors we speculate about aren't distant beings from other planets, but rather spiritual entities—angels or demons—acting within the divine cosmic drama outlined in Scripture? This leads us to a critical exploration we'll address in the next chapter, where we delve deeper into the idea that these ancient beings could be manifesting in our modern world in forms we interpret as extraterrestrial.

Looking Ahead

The possibility of extraterrestrial life has sparked debate for more than a thousand years, among scholars ranging from medieval philosophers to modern theologians. These discussions challenge believers to explore life beyond Earth and how it intersects with Christian theology, particularly regarding the incarnation, redemption, and renewal of all creation.

Yet, as intriguing as the idea of extraterrestrial life may be, we must ask: Is this the most plausible explanation for the visitors many claim to encounter today? Could these beings be something more familiar—not from distant planets, but from another realm entirely? Scripture frequently references spiritual beings—angels, demons, and other entities—that have long interacted with humanity. These beings could fit more naturally into the biblical narrative of cosmic conflict and divine intervention.

As we reflect on this, we must consider: Are what some perceive as extraterrestrial visitors actually spiritual entities with purposes aligned with or opposed to God's plans? Could angels or demons be manifesting in ways that resonate with our modern expectations of extraterrestrials?

Scripture encourages discernment. Ephesians 6:12 reminds us our battle is "against the rulers, against the authorities, against the powers of this dark world and against the spiritual forces of evil in the heavenly realms." These truths call us to approach the phenomenon of extraterrestrial life with curiosity, but also with caution, always grounded in the supremacy of Christ.

Whether we're encountering beings from other planets or spiritual entities from unseen realms, one truth remains central: Christ is Lord over all creation. Colossians 1:16 affirms: "For by Him all things were created: things in heaven and on earth, visible and invisible." No matter how vast or mysterious the cosmos, it remains under Christ's sovereign rule, whose redemptive love reaches every corner of existence.

In the next chapter, we will explore whether these visitors might not be extraterrestrials at all, but spiritual beings—angels or demons—who have long played a crucial role in the biblical narrative and may now be manifesting in ways that speak to our modern age.

Chapter 11

THE GOD WE TRUST: DISCERNING THE SPIRITUAL WAR BEHIND THE UFO PHENOMENON

> How has it happened, sir, that we have not hitherto once
> thought of humbly applying to the Father of Lights to illu-
> minate our understanding?
>
> —BENJAMIN FRANKLIN

> All the miseries and evils which men suffer…proceed from
> their despising or neglecting the precepts contained in the
> Bible.
>
> —NOAH WEBSTER

> The war is inevitable—and let it come! I repeat it, sir, let
> it come!
>
> —PATRICK HENRY

The Bible offers a rich supernatural worldview that provides a clearer lens by which to understand the UFO phenomenon than do modern scientific or cultural explanations. Stories of "high strangeness"—a term used to describe bizarre or unexplained phenomena, such as UFOs, UAPs, or humanoid visitors—aren't new to human experience. Throughout Scripture, divine beings interact with humans in ways that resonate with modern reports of extraterrestrial encounters. Just as the Founding Fathers trusted in the God of the Bible when contemplating the vast mysteries of the cosmos, we, too, must look to Scripture for answers. Their unwavering faith in the Creator's sovereignty, extending beyond the earth to the heavens, serves as a powerful model for us today as we navigate the growing flood of UFO reports. In an age of confusion and deception, the Bible offers not only insight but protection, reminding us that the true spiritual battle is one that transcends the physical. This chapter will explore how the supernatural worldview of the Bible, steeped in angelic and demonic manifestations, accounts for much of what society attributes to extraterrestrial visitors.

Encounters with the Visitors

Communion, a book written by Whitley Strieber and published in 1987, brought alien abduction into mainstream consciousness. Strieber recounted his own alleged abduction experiences in this controversial work that became a bestseller, sparking widespread debate about extraterrestrial contact. It significantly influenced popular culture, with its chilling accounts of nonhuman entities interacting with humans. While some readers were skeptical, others found the narrative compelling, believing Strieber's encounters mirrored their own experiences.

We've already detailed well-known abduction cases earlier in the book, such as the Pascagoula River incident, the Travis Walton abduction, the Ariel School encounter, and the experiences of Betty and Barney Hill. These accounts, coming in from the quiet Mississippi riverbanks to the forests of Arizona, reveal the global and disturbing nature of these abductions. Can the Bible really explain such unusual encounters with non-human beings? Surprisingly, yes. This is illustrated by the fall of angels—celestial beings who rebelled and became the mysterious forces engaging with humanity from ancient times to modern abduction phenomena. These encounters may not be isolated events, but rather part of a greater cosmic struggle, one that's been unfolding since the dawn of creation.

The Watchers and the Biblical View of Supernatural Beings

One of the most compelling and mysterious narratives within the broader biblical tradition is the tale of the Watchers—angels who sinned by taking human wives. Found in Genesis 6:1–4 and in the Jewish book of 1 Enoch 6, this story has intrigued scholars and laypeople alike, spawning extensive theological discourse and speculative interpretations. In previous books, I've written extensively about the Watchers/Sons of God narrative, examining its biblical roots, its expansion in extrabiblical texts, and even its Mesopotamian backdrop.

Let's first examine Genesis 6:1–4, where the account of the Watchers begins succinctly. The passage describes how the "sons of God" saw that the daughters of humans were beautiful and took them as wives, leading to the birth of the Nephilim, a race of giants. This union was a direct violation of divine order, resulting in widespread corruption and setting the stage for the Great Flood.

> When human beings began to increase in number on the earth and daughters were born to them, the sons of God saw that the daughters of humans were beautiful, and they married any of them they chose. Then the Lord said, "My Spirit will not contend with humans forever, for they are mortal; their days will be a hundred and twenty years." The Nephilim were on the earth in those days—and also afterward—when the sons of God went to the daughters of humans and had children by them. They were the heroes of old, men of renown. (Genesis 6:1–4, NIV)

The term "sons of God" (*benê ha'elohîm*) refers to an elder race of divine beings that predate humanity. This interpretation is supported by other Old Testament passages, such as Job 1:6 and Job 2:1, where the same term is used to describe heavenly beings presenting themselves before God and attending the creation event. The actions of some of these beings—taking human wives and producing the

Nephilim—represent a significant transgression against the established divine order.

The "sons of God" are the primary instigators, whose lust and desire for human women lead them to abandon their heavenly station. The human women, referred to as the "daughters of men," are the recipients of this divine attention, and their union with the angels results in the birth of the Nephilim. The Nephilim, described as "heroes of old, men of renown," are a hybrid race of giants whose presence on earth contributes to the increasing wickedness and corruption of humanity. This rebellion and the resulting corruption prompt God to limit the lifespan of humanity to 120 years, signaling the impending divine judgment. This judgment culminates in the Great Flood, a cataclysmic event intended to cleanse the earth of its pervasive sin and restore order.

The brevity of the Genesis account leaves much to the imagination, prompting various interpretations and expansions in later Jewish literature (such as 1 Enoch, Jubilees).

The Book of Enoch

The Book of Enoch, a collection of ancient Jewish apocalyptic writings, provides an expanded account of the Watchers' rebellion. This text, particularly 1 Enoch 6–11, offers detailed descriptions of the events and characters involved, adding layers of complexity and nuance to the Genesis narrative.

In the Book of Enoch, the Watchers descend to Mount Hermon from their heavenly post, where they swear an oath to carry out their plan together. This collective decision underscores the magnitude of their rebellion, as they knowingly defy divine command to fulfill their desires.

> And it came to pass when the children of men had multiplied that in those days were born unto them beautiful and comely daughters. And the angels, the children of the heaven, saw and lusted after them, and said to one another: "Come, let us choose us wives from among the children of men and beget us children."

And Semjaza, who was their leader, said unto them: "I fear ye will not indeed agree to do this deed, and I alone shall have to pay the penalty of a great sin." And they all answered him and said: "Let us all swear an oath, and all bind ourselves by mutual imprecations not to abandon this plan but to do this thing." Then sware they all together and bound themselves by mutual imprecations upon it. (1 Enoch 6:1–6)

The Watchers' actions result in the birth of the Nephilim, who are depicted as giants with great strength and influence. These beings further corrupt humanity, teaching them forbidden knowledge and practices, including the use of magic, astrology, and metallurgy.

And Azazel taught men to make swords, and knives, and shields, and breastplates, and made known to them the metals of the earth and the art of working them, and bracelets, and orna-ments, and the use of antimony, and the beautifying of the eyelids, and all kinds of costly stones, and all coloring tinctures. And there arose much godlessness, and they committed forni-cation, and they were led astray, and became corrupt in all their ways. (1 Enoch 8:1–3)

In addition to their illicit unions, the Watchers are credited with imparting forbidden knowledge to humans, including the arts of magic, metallurgy, and other esoteric sciences, thereby accelerating humanity's descent into sin and chaos.

Ancient Aliens? The Watchers in Mesopotamian Lore

The historical stories of the Bible didn't happen in a vacuum. The Genesis 6:1–4 narrative was also preserved by the Mesopotamians. The Apkallu, or "sages," are significant figures in Mesopotamian mythology, often depicted as wise beings who brought essential knowledge to human-ity. These beings, part human and part fish or bird, were considered intermediaries between the gods and humans, imparting critical cultural and scientific knowledge.

The Apkallu emerged from the Apsu, the primeval waters, and served the god Ea (Enki), the deity of wisdom and water. They were revered as culture heroes who provided civilization's essential arts and sciences, including writing, agriculture, and building. The Apkallu were seen as bearers of divine knowledge, tasked with guiding humanity and ensuring the preservation of culture and wisdom.

The parallels between the Apkallu and the Watchers are striking: Both groups brought advanced knowledge to humanity before the Flood and were associated with transgressions that led to significant consequences. The Apkallu, sent to instruct humanity but later contributing to its corruption, mirrors the Watchers teaching forbidden knowledge and leading humanity astray. In Jewish/Christian tradition as well as Mesopotamian mythology, these divine beings imparted knowledge, but ultimately faced punishment for their transgressions in the abyss (1 Enoch 10:4–6; 2 Peter 2:4; Jude 1:6). Any beings associated with the UFO/UAP phenomenon should take note.

This shared motif reflects a broader cultural concern with the boundaries between the divine and human realms and the consequences of crossing those boundaries. By taking human wives and imparting forbidden knowledge, the Watchers violated the natural order, disrupting the balance of creation and necessitating divine intervention in the form of the Flood.

Ancient vs. Modern: Spiritual Beings and UFO Phenomena

The Watchers narrative provides a historical and theological context that can shed light on those contacted by a visiting presence.

Appearance and adaptation: Angelic beings possess the ability to alter their appearance to suit different contexts and times. In modern encounters, the "visitors" often exhibit physical forms that align with Hollywood imagery of extraterrestrials, such as the Greys, Reptilians, and Insectilins. This adaptability could be a strategic choice, allowing them to interact with humans in a manner that fits the prevailing cultural narratives and expectations. But it raises a profound question: Are these beings appearing as extraterrestrials because that's how we expect them to look, or is our media subtly reflecting a more profound truth about their existence? As human culture and technology evolve, so, too, do the forms and narratives of these beings, mirroring our current fears, hopes, and curiosities.

Technological manifestation: In ancient times, the Watchers imparted forbidden knowledge such as metallurgy and astrology. Today, their manifestation as technologically advanced beings could be seen as a continuation of their role as knowledge-bearers, now providing insights into advanced technology and cosmic phenomena.

Observation and experimentation: Angels could be engaged in long-term observation and experimentation, studying human responses to their presence and the knowledge they impart.

Redemption or control: Some angels might seek to rectify their past transgressions by guiding humanity towards a certain path of enlightenment or technological advancement. This was true in 1 Enoch when they asked Enoch to plead with Yahweh to let them out of the abyss. This could explain some positive encounters with the phenomenon. While I am personally very skeptical of this view, it cannot be ruled out.

Testing boundaries: Encounters described by some experiencers can be interpreted as a form of boundary testing, probing the limits of human understanding and tolerance for the unknown. By presenting themselves in various forms and inducing a range of emotional and psychological responses, they might be assessing humanity's readiness for greater revelations or contact.

Spiritual warfare: From a theological perspective, the actions of these beings should be viewed as part of a broader cosmic struggle between forces of good and evil. Their presence and influence are undoubtedly intended to challenge human faith, sow confusion, or test moral and spiritual resilience.

As previously mentioned, Whitley Strieber's *Communion* played a pivotal role in bringing alien abduction into the cultural spotlight. In *Them*, a separate book by Strieber that explores other people's encounters with these entities, he dives deeper into the transformative impact of such experiences. In chapter 7 of that book, a witness describes feeling fundamentally changed after an encounter with the visitors, experiencing a profound sense of renewal and personal growth. Strieber analyzes the psychological and emotional transformations resulting from these interactions, suggesting these encounters can catalyze personal development and spiritual awakening.[91] He even posits that the visitors might play a role in facilitating human evolution or expanding consciousness.

Another witness in the book recounts a spiritually profound encounter, feeling a deep sense of unity and interconnectedness with the cosmos. Strieber explores the idea that these experiences can shift one's worldview, suggesting that the visitors may act as catalysts for personal and collective transformation, elevating human consciousness and fostering interconnectedness.[92] In chapter 9, a witness feels initiated into a larger cosmic narrative, as if being prepared for a greater purpose.[93] Strieber examines the notion that these encounters are part of a larger plan, potentially providing insight into the visitors' motives and guiding humanity toward a deeper understanding of its place in the universe. None of these experiences are likely to prod the experiencers to open their Bible and trust in God; rather, it gives a false sense of security and peace that the universe or the visitors can't offer—it can only be given in Jesus Christ. This is clever spiritual warfare.

Strieber also describes a family that grapples with the impact of a child's encounters with visitors. The child describes seeing strange beings in their room, causing fear and confusion. Initially skeptical, the parents eventually witness the phenomena themselves, leading to tension and fear within the household and straining family dynamics.[94] Strieber explores the psychological effects of these experiences on both the child and the family, highlighting the challenges of integrating such encounters into everyday life. He emphasizes the need for support and understanding within families to cope with the potential long-term psychological effects of these occurrences. Indeed, the visitor's resume of evoking negative emotions by contactees is long. This screams "demonic." In the context of UFOs, these "fallen angels" or "gods" could be seen as continuing their interaction with humanity, but under a new guise: No longer openly worshiped as mere deities, they now manifest as beings from the stars, or extraterrestrials.

Divine Aerial Signs and Modern Deception: Biblical Parallels to UFOs?

Making a general assessment that aliens are demonic entities presents certain challenges. After all, do angels construct UFOs? Do demons pilot them? It sounds peculiar when said aloud. However, the Bible features numerous accounts of supernatural aerial phenomena—manifestations of divine power that, at first glance, resemble what we might now describe as UFOs. Yet, these biblical events stand in stark contrast to the UFO phenomenon observed today, which I assert is rooted in deception and darkness. In each biblical instance, the aerial occurrences are directed by God's sovereign will, showcasing His ultimate authority over creation. Consider the following examples:

1. **The pillar of cloud and fire (Exodus 13:21–22):** This divine manifestation led the Israelites through the wilderness. By day, a cloud moved ahead; by night, a pillar of fire provided light. Its controlled flight and light emission illustrate God's use of the aerial realm to guide and protect His people.

2. **Ezekiel's vision (Ezekiel 1):** In one of Scripture's most vivid supernatural encounters, Ezekiel saw a whirlwind, angelic creatures, and "wheels within wheels" that moved with intelligence and divine purpose. While some have attempted to modernize this as a UFO sighting, the biblical context reveals this as a holy encounter with God's angelic agents, not a deceptive phenomenon.

3. **Elijah's ascension (2 Kings 2:11):** Elijah was taken up to heaven in a chariot of fire, a supernatural event orchestrated by God. While modern accounts of individuals being taken up by unknown craft exist, Elijah's ascension was a divine act of translation into heaven, not an abduction by sinister forces.

4. **The star of Bethlehem (Matthew 2:1–12):** The star that led the wise men to Jesus' birthplace is another divine aerial sign. Unlike the malevolent light phenomena associated with modern UFO encounters, this star was a beacon of divine revelation, guiding humanity toward God's redemptive plan.

These biblical accounts aren't just stories of unexplained lights in the sky, but are manifestations of God's control over the aerial realm. In each case, these events are deeply tied to God's redemptive plan, emphasizing His mercy, guidance, and sovereignty.

However, the UFO occurrences we witness today are something entirely different. Although there may be superficial similarities, such as lights or flying objects, these encounters are not divine but demonic in nature. The Bible emphasizes that the spirit realm has aerial capabilities beyond human comprehension, and these powers are not limited to the forces of good. Satan, as the "prince of the power of the air" (Ephesians 2:2), exercises influence over the aerial realms, using them to deceive and manipulate humanity. What we see unfolding today echoes the agenda of the fallen angels in Genesis 6, where their interaction with humanity was aimed at corruption and destruction.

Jesus Himself warned that the last days would be like the days of Noah (Matthew 24:37), a time marked by unprecedented spiritual rebellion and deception. The parallels are unmistakable: Just as the fallen angels of Genesis 6 sought to corrupt humanity through illicit means, so, too, does the modern UFO phenomenon mirror their destructive agenda. The mysterious crashes of supposed extraterrestrial craft— events skeptics find puzzling—may very well be intentional "donations" by dark forces, aimed at leading nations to reverse engineer dangerous technologies.

The purpose behind this is not advancement but escalation, pushing humanity toward its own destruction by weaponizing these technologies. It's Genesis 6 all over again—a scheme to undermine humankind by technological and spiritual means. The battle for the aerial realm is as old as time, and while today's phenomena may seem novel, they are but a continuation of the spiritual warfare that has been raging since the beginning. We must recognize that what's happening in the skies isn't just a technological marvel, but a spiritual deception with eternal stakes. This becomes even more apparent when we examine the deeply unsettling subject of alien abduction.

The Data Points to Demons

The phenomenon of alien abduction has captured the public's attention for decades, not merely through sensationalized media, but through the harrowing testimonies of countless individuals. These narratives—striking in their uniformity—recount stories of beings, ostensibly extraterrestrial, who abduct, probe, and leave their human victims with lingering physical and psychological scars. While many have dismissed these accounts as fabrications or psychological delusions, they persist, prompting researchers to explore their origins from various angles.

In 2011, researchers Denise Stoner and Kathleen Marden undertook a meticulous study to identify commonalities among those who reported such experiences. Building upon the foundations laid by scholars like David Jacobs, PhD, and John Mack, MD, they sought to uncover patterns that might reveal deeper truths about these phenomena.

They discovered a staggering 64 percent of those who quantified their abductions reported being taken more than ten times, often starting in childhood. This suggests the abduction phenomenon is an ongoing process, not a one-time event. Most abductees (88 percent) had conscious recall of at least one abduction. Seventy-six percent indicated they were not alone when they were taken, and 62 percent of the witnesses had conscious recall for at least part of the experience. This high level of recall, coupled with the presence of witnesses, lends credibility to the abductees' accounts, suggesting these experiences aren't mere psychological or physiological disturbances. Significantly, 67 percent of abductees recalled seeing an unconventional craft at less than one thousand feet before an abduction, and 56 percent recalled seeing nonhuman entities immediately before being taken. Additionally, 58 percent were aware of having been examined aboard an alien craft. These findings suggest the abductions are characterized by recurring experiences consistent among different individuals.[95]

"Alien" encounters may not be extraterrestrial at all, but encounters with demonic entities as described in Scripture. The physiological and paranormal incidents reported further suggest a demonic origin. The study found that 83 percent of abductees woke up with unexplained marks on their bodies. These marks—often bruises, puncture wounds, or rashes—mirror the physical effects seen in cases of demonic oppression (Mark 9:25–26). Furthermore, 69 percent of female abductees reported gynecological problems. Many gave accounts of suffering from migraines, chronic fatigue syndrome, and emotional turmoil—including anxiety, fear, and difficulty sleeping.[96]

Paranormal activity was also prevalent, with 88 percent of abductees reporting light orbs, poltergeist activity, and unexplained noises in their homes—details strikingly similar to traditional descriptions of demonic presence (Ephesians 6:12).[97] The development of psychic abilities following these experiences further supports the idea of demonic manipulation. Many reported gaining new abilities such as telepathy and clairvoyance after their encounters, possibly the result of demonic influence (Acts 16:16–18; 2 Thessalonians 2:9–10). These disturbances suggest the entities involved aren't merely visiting from another planet, but are actively seeking to invade and disrupt the lives of their victims (Mark 5:1–20). Moreover, the fact that these disturbances occur in the homes of abductees suggests the entities aren't bound by physical limitations and are capable of exerting their influence over a prolonged period. This is consistent with the behavior of demons as described in Scripture, where they're often depicted as persistent and relentless in their efforts to torment and deceive their victims (Ephesians 6:12).

When viewed through the lens of demonology, the abduction phenomenon can be understood as part of a larger spiritual battle between the forces of good and evil (Ephesians 6:12). The entities that present themselves as extraterrestrial beings may actually be demonic, using the guise of aliens to further their malevolent agenda. By convincing humanity that these encounters are the result of advanced alien civilizations, the demons divert attention away from the true nature of the spiritual battle and lead people farther away from God.

The data collected by Stoner and Marden strongly supports a Christian interpretation that abduction experiences are encounters with demonic entities, not extraterrestrial beings. The prevalence of paranormal activity, physical and psychological effects, and psychic phenomena among abductees aligns closely with a demonic profile. As we will see next, the phenomenon being demonic is exactly what some government insiders believe as well.

Memo 6751: A Glimpse into a Declassified Document on Roswell

As we delve deeper into the intersection of the supernatural worldview of the Bible and the modern UFO phenomenon, it's essential to consider pivotal historical documents that shed light on how governmental and military authorities have engaged with these enigmatic occurrences. One such document is Memo 6751, a declassified government memorandum dated July 8, 1947, written shortly after the infamous Roswell incident. This document can be accessed directly on the FBI's website.[98]

Memo 6751 discusses the nature of the "flying discs" now commonly referred to as UFOs or UAPs. The note, addressed to various scientists, aeronautic, and military authorities, suggests these discs aren't merely advanced technological crafts, but may have a supernatural or otherworldly origin. The author of the memo, whose identity remains anonymous, raises several points that resonate with the supernatural worldview described in the Bible:

1. **Non-earthly origin of the visitors**: The memo asserts that these "visitors" are not from Earth. It states they don't come from any "planet," as we use this word, but from an ethereal plane that is imperceptible to us.

2. **Humanoid appearance, but superior size**: The memo describes the visitors as humanoid, but significantly larger than humans.

3. **Peaceful mission**: The memo mentions that the visitors' mission is peaceful, and that they are possibly contemplating settling on Earth.

4. **Advanced technology beyond human comprehension**: The memo highlights that these discs possess a type of radiant energy or ray capable of disintegrating any attacking force.

5. **Esoteric and spiritual interpretations**: Interestingly, the memo also references concepts such as "Lokas" and "Talas," terms that are rooted in esoteric traditions. They may allude to different planes of existence or realms within the spiritual hierarchy, further suggesting that the phenomenon might be interacting with humanity from a nonphysical realm, akin to the spirit world described in the Bible.[99]

Memo 6751 isn't merely a relic of mid-twentieth-century UFO hysteria, but a significant document that bridges modern governmental concerns with the ancient supernatural worldview of the Bible. The document's content suggests that at least some individuals within the US government were willing to consider the possibility that these phenomena might not be of this world, but instead belong to a spiritual or otherworldly domain—much like the divine beings and occurrences described in Scripture.

This memo serves as a tangible connection between ancient biblical narratives and modern accounts of high strangeness. It reinforces the notion that what we now classify as UFOs/UAPs may have roots in the same supernatural traditions the Bible addresses—beings from other realms, interacting with humanity, and influencing the course of history. Memo 6751 provides a crucial piece of evidence that the boundary between the human and the divine—or the physical and the spiritual—remains as permeable today as it was in biblical times.

The Collins Elite: A Shadow Power in UAP Investigations

Within the depths of the Pentagon and the intelligence community, a covert group known as the Collins Elite has long remained hidden, operating at the intersection of religion, national security, and the unexplained. Their existence was largely whispered about in the halls of government and was dismissed by many as conspiracy. However, as revealed by Luis Elizondo in his book *Imminent*, this secretive circle of religious fundamentalists wasn't just a rumor; they were real, and their influence over US policy—particularly regarding UAPs—was undeniable.[100]

The Collins Elite wielded significant power within the US defense apparatus, shaping policy decisions behind the scenes. Yet, their motivations set them apart from other military and intelligence factions. Rather than approaching UAPs through a lens of science or national security, the Collins Elite viewed these phenomena as manifestations of a much older, spiritual struggle—one that extended far beyond mere technology. For them, the UFO occurrences were tied to forces more demonic than extraterrestrial, and their mission was to ensure that the US government didn't inadvertently open doors to spiritual dangers. As Elizondo notes in *Imminent*, his initial reaction to hearing about the Collins Elite was one of skepticism. The idea that a religious faction could operate within the Pentagon, shaping policy based on theological rather than empirical beliefs, seemed far-fetched. However, as Elizondo would come to learn, the group's influence was very real, and their ability to affect UAP investigations was significant. Luis, referred to by the nickname "Lue," reveals the following conversation he had with one of these Pentagon insiders:

"Lue, you know we already know what these things are, right?"

I wasn't sure if Woods was asking a question or making a statement. "I'm sorry, sir," I said. "What are you specifically referring to?"

I sensed his annoyance. Deep in my mind, I secretly hoped Woods knew something I didn't. I hoped Woods would reveal to me that these UAP we hunted were actually some sort of secret US technology, hidden deep within the black budgets of the Defense Advanced Research Projects Agency (DARPA) or the Air Force Research Laboratory (AFRL). That would have been a welcome relief.

"Have you read your Bible lately, Lue?" he asked.

"Um…sir, I am familiar with the Bible," I said. What a strange thing to ask, I thought.

"Lue, you're opening a can of worms playing with this stuff," Woods said.

It was clear to me he was talking about UAP. I can't imagine the look on my face. But I'm sure Woods could tell I was perplexed.

"It's demonic," he said to me. "There is no reason we should be looking into this. We already know what they are and where they come from. They are deceivers. Demons."

I couldn't believe what I was hearing. This was a senior intelligence official putting his religious beliefs ahead of national security.[101]

The Collins Elite's members were deeply embedded within the Pentagon and intelligence community, many of them holding senior positions for decades. Their anonymity was their greatest strength; they moved quietly and operated without drawing attention, shaping policy through whispers, private meetings, and strategic influence.

While many in government, including Elizondo and other members of AATIP, approached the UAP issue from a secular, data-driven standpoint, the Collins Elite saw the investigation as something dangerous—physically and spiritually. They feared that looking too deeply into UAPs could lead to an engagement with demonic forces, opening doors that couldn't easily be closed. As a result, they worked tirelessly to halt or derail UAP investigations whenever possible.

The true power of the Collins Elite lay not in their numbers or formal authority, but in their ability to influence decision-makers. They weren't a formal department or agency; they had no official title. Yet their reach extended far beyond what most would imagine. They were insiders, often occupying key roles within the Pentagon and the intelligence community. Many had spent their entire careers within the halls of government, rising through the ranks and earning the trust of senior officials.

Their influence was subtle but effective. They didn't need public recognition or formal positions to shape policy. As Elizondo describes, they were capable of killing programs and halting investigations with a well-placed conversation or a strategic whisper in the ear of a powerful figure. Their power was not to be underestimated, despite the fact that most people—inside and outside of government—had never heard of them.

The Collins Elite's primary focus was to prevent UAP investigations from veering too far into dangerous spiritual territory. They believed any attempt to engage with or understand UAPs from a purely scientific perspective was foolhardy, as it missed the greater spiritual threat posed by these phenomena. To them, the investigation of UAPs could lead to occult practices, demonic influence, or worse. Their mission wasn't just to safeguard national security, but to protect the nation's spiritual health.

Looking Ahead

As we begin to understand that these modern encounters aren't extraterrestrial, but demonic in nature, it's important to recognize that deception is nothing new. From the earliest days of human civilization, the forces of darkness have been laying the groundwork for this grand deception, using curiosity as their primary tool for manipulation. What follows is a deeper exploration of this strategy, which has been ages in the making, and how it continues to unfold in our time. In the next chapter, we will evaluate the "Alien Manifesto"—a modern doctrine that cleverly disguises ancient lies under the guise of cosmic enlightenment. Through careful examination, we'll see how these so-called revelations echo the deceptions of old, aiming to lead humanity farther away from the truth of the gospel and deeper into spiritual confusion. This manifesto is not merely an alien message, but a calculated step in the spiritual warfare we now face.

Chapter 12

THE ALIEN AGENDA:
UNVEILING THE STRATEGY OF COSMIC DELUSION

Tyranny, like hell, is not easily conquered.

—THOMAS PAINE

From the beginning of human civilization, powerful forces have sought to manipulate the course of history. Their greatest weapon has been deception, and now, in our age of UFO sightings and government disclosures, the layers of that deception are beginning to be peeled back. At the heart of this lies what I call the "Alien Constitution"—an ancient and insidious framework designed not by beings from distant stars, but by spiritual forces intent on leading humanity astray.

This Alien Constitution is not a physical document; it is a binding agreement—a cosmic contract of rebellion that exploits our deepest curiosities and unanswered questions about life beyond Earth. Just as our nation's founding Constitution shaped the laws and direction of America, this alien constitution has established the terms of deception, setting the stage for a global rebellion that will culminate in the final days. As these deceptions intensify, so, too, does the spiritual battle that wages in unseen realms, drawing humanity closer to the fulfillment of end-times prophecy.

This chapter seeks to unveil the nature of that constitution. We will explore how this hidden agenda, seeded in ancient times, now finds new expression in the UFO phenomenon. We will examine how these modern encounters mirror the tactics used by the fallen Watchers, who, in ancient days, offered forbidden knowledge to humankind, and how the same manipulation is at play today—cloaked in the guise of extraterrestrial contact.

The Alien Constitution isn't merely about UFOs or government secrets; it represents a cosmic rebellion against God's authority. As this ancient agenda reveals itself in modern skies, we face a crucial question: Will we recognize the spiritual war unfolding around us, or succumb to the deception that has been millennia in the making? The answer will determine more than our understanding—it will shape our eternal destiny.

What follows is a deeper exploration of this age-old strategy, revealing how it continues to unfold in our time, and the profound implications it carries for humanity's future.

Curiosity as a Tool for Manipulation

Curiosity, humanity's greatest asset, is also its most vulnerable point. While it drives progress and exploration, it also opens the door to manipulation by unseen forces. The Watchers exploited this trait by offering forbidden knowledge—sorcery, astrology, and warfare. They disguised themselves as benefactors, using humanity's thirst for knowledge to corrupt and lead mankind away from the divine order.

The UFO phenomenon follows the same manipulative pattern. These entities play upon humanity's yearning to understand extraterrestrial life, presenting themselves as purveyors of higher knowledge. They promise to unlock the universe's secrets, posing as benevolent guides ready to usher in an age of technological and spiritual enlightenment. However, beneath the guise of wisdom lies a sinister purpose. Their ultimate goal, much like the Watchers of old, is to lead humanity away

164

from God and deeper into rebellion against His divine order. The consistent use of curiosity as a weapon of deceit suggests a longstanding plan, patiently waiting for the right moment to lead humanity astray.

God's Silence: A Strategic Cosmic Test?

Yves Congar, a French Dominican friar, priest, and theologian who was later made a cardinal by Pope John Paul II, is remembered for his famous remark about the purpose of the early chapters of Genesis: "Scripture's goal is to teach us the way to Heaven, not the workings of the heavens."[102] In his appendix titled "Has God Peopled the Stars?" from *The Wide World My Parish*, Congar stated, "Christian doctrine does not concern itself with stars or the existence of other inhabited worlds, but rather with Heaven." He further noted that since Revelation doesn't address the issue, Christians are free to speculate whether other worlds are inhabited or not, as "biblically speaking, it is an entirely open question."[103] He concluded by saying that "theology finds no difficulty" with the possibility of extraterrestrial intelligence.

In the cosmic battle for humanity's soul, God's silence on the existence of otherworldly beings is not an oversight—it may be a test of faith. This divine silence forces people to trust in the sufficiency of God's revelation and resist the temptation to seek answers beyond His Word. However, the forces of darkness have long understood how to exploit this silence. Much like the fallen angels, who capitalized on humankind's uncertainty by offering forbidden knowledge, today's UFO entities take advantage of the void of silence, crafting deceptive narratives.

By stepping into this silence, these entities create false cosmologies that challenge the biblical account of creation and humanity's role in the universe. They present themselves as higher intelligences offering answers that undermine God's authority and lead humanity to question the sufficiency of divine revelation. The powers of darkness have been subtly planning this for ages, crafting a scheme that now challenges the very foundations of biblical truth.

The Bible provides warnings about spiritual deception in the last days. Matthew 24:24 warns of false prophets and false messiahs who would "perform great signs and wonders" to deceive even the elect, if possible. Similarly, 2 Thessalonians 2:9–11 speaks of "the coming of the lawless one" as being "in accordance with how Satan works," using "all sorts of displays of power through signs and wonders that serve the lie." These warnings remind us that such deceptions aren't merely the product of human curiosity, but part of a larger spiritual strategy to lead humanity astray.

The Hidden Agenda: Hybridization and Surveillance

The UFO phenomenon, which began with mere sightings, has steadily evolved into a calculated operation meticulously orchestrated by the powers of darkness. Early UFO encounters, like those in Roswell and Washington, DC, were only the beginning. These events captured the public's imagination and fostered curiosity, but they were part of a larger, long-term plan to manipulate humanity's understanding of the cosmos and its place within it.

Over time, this effort has intensified. Reports of extraterrestrial biological entities and abductions indicate these encounters have evolved from mere anomalies to direct biological interactions. Many echo the ancient accounts of fallen angels before the Flood, who interfered with human genetics to create the Nephilim—the earlier-mentioned race of giants described in Genesis and the Book of Enoch. Today's "visitors" are reported to be conducting hybridization experiments and manipulating the very fabric of human life.

But what is the true purpose behind a breeding program?

One theory suggests these entities are preparing for the final battle foretold in Scripture. Revelation 16:14 describes demonic spirits gathering the kings of the world for war on the great day of God Almighty. By creating hybrids—part human, part something else—these entities could be forming a legion that is neither fully human nor fully spiritual,

166

but something in between: a force bred for warfare, deception, and rebellion. This aligns with the ancient warnings about the Nephilim, whose existence corrupted humanity before the Flood.

A disturbing possibility is that hybrids are being planted across the galaxy, awaiting discovery. Such discoveries could trigger a crisis of belief, challenging humanity's unique place in God's creation and undermining faith in the biblical narrative. These discoveries would promote false cosmologies that question Christ's role as the sole Redeemer, creating alternative origin stories that divert people from Scripture. This deception could lead to a global crisis of faith, tempting many to seek answers outside of God's Word and embrace a deceptive worldview that opposes the truth of the Gospel.

Another unsettling possibility is that these entities are actively gathering intelligence on humanity, with hybrids already walking among us as covert operatives—eyes and ears planted to monitor our every move. The hybridization experiments may serve as a form of reconnaissance, allowing these beings to better understand human biology, psychology, and even spiritual vulnerabilities. By blending in, they could gather invaluable information to manipulate or control humankind in future events, much like how military powers conduct surveillance before launching larger operations.

These hybrids, potentially indistinguishable from the rest of us, might be embedded within society, collecting data not just on our physical traits, but on how we think, believe, and worship. Such insights could later be exploited to weaken our faith and prepare the world for a grand deception or even direct conflict. In this scenario, the ultimate goal of the surveillance isn't just intelligence-gathering, but the groundwork for a future attempt to influence, control, or deceive humanity on a global scale.

Time Travelers: The Future Human Theory

Another recent theory, advanced in a speculative Harvard study, suggests that the entities involved in UFO sightings and encounters may not be extraterrestrial at all, but rather evolved *future humans*.[104] This hypothesis, known as the "extratempestrial theory," posits that these beings are descendants of Earth's future population, having developed the ability to traverse time. According to this view, they aren't alien visitors from a distant galaxy, but time travelers, studying their evolutionary past—our present—through the lens of advanced technology.

One of the leading voices in this theory is Dr. Michael P. Masters, a biological anthropologist and author of *Identified Flying Objects: A Multidisciplinary Scientific Approach to the UFO Phenomenon and the Extratempestrial Model*. Masters, an experiencer himself, has revealed that his encounters with the phenomenon have shaped his theories. In one unsettling interaction, Masters recounts how the entities communicated with him, suggesting, "You know what we are, don't you?" This personal revelation, coupled with his academic expertise, led Masters to theorize that these visitors could be our own future descendants—studying us through the prism of evolutionary anthropology.

While intriguing, this theory presents a profound spiritual risk. By framing these beings as simply future versions of humanity, the narrative shifts from one of creation and prophetic eschatology to evolution and technological determinism. It removes the urgency of Christ's imminent return, replacing it with a materialistic belief that humanity's destiny is in its own hands. If the entities visiting us are simply our evolved future selves, the focus drifts away from preparing for the Second Coming of Jesus to a narrative centered on human progress and mastery over time. This subtle shift can numb spiritual vigilance, leading people to believe the future isn't shaped by divine intervention, but by human evolution and technological advancements.

Looking Ahead

As we close this chapter on the strategy of cosmic delusion, it becomes clear that the UFO phenomenon isn't just a modern mystery or a matter of extraterrestrial contact—it is spiritual warfare on a cosmic scale.

Deception, deeply rooted in humanity's history, has now evolved into a global strategy, using the allure of the unknown to mislead many. The forces of darkness are orchestrating this end-times deception, manipulating our curiosity and reshaping our understanding of the universe.

But as the veil of secrecy continues to unravel, the question becomes not only about what these entities are, but why now? This grand deception, once lurking in the shadows, is poised to make its most significant move yet. As world leaders face mounting pressure to disclose the truth about these encounters, the ultimate test of humanity's faith and understanding is about to be laid bare.

The next chapter will explore this seismic shift in more detail, profiling "The Disclosure President"—the one who will stand before the world and unveil the truth that will change Earth and humanity forever. Yet, this revelation isn't just political or scientific—it is a spiritual reckoning. Prepare for the unveiling of not only information, but the very heart of a cosmic battle that will challenge humanity's faith in ways we've never before imagined.

Chapter 13

THE DISCLOSURE PRESIDENT:
UNVEILING THE TRUTH THAT WILL CHANGE EARTH
AND HUMANITY FOREVER

I know no safe depository of the ultimate powers of the society but the people themselves; and if we think them not enlightened enough to exercise their control with a wholesome discretion, the remedy is not to take it from them, but to inform their discretion by education. This is the true corrective of abuses of constitutional power.

—THOMAS JEFFERSON

As we move closer to the possibility of an official disclosure, it's essential to consider the kind of leader who will deliver such an earth-shattering announcement. This future president will carry the profound responsibility of guiding humanity into a new era—one in which extraterrestrial contact is openly acknowledged. Unlike the cautious approaches of the past, this leader will have no choice but to face the truth head-on, understanding that secrecy can no longer be maintained in the face of overwhelming evidence.

Historically, American presidents have been privy to some of the nation's deepest secrets. Harry Truman, for example, had to oversee the creation of the CIA and grapple with the early, mysterious sightings like the Roswell incident in 1947, navigating public and military pressure while safeguarding national security. In a similar vein, Dwight D. Eisenhower was rumored to have had covert meetings with extraterrestrial beings, a speculation that hints at how deeply secrecy surrounding these topics runs, even at the highest levels. These historical moments echo the profound responsibility future presidents will face when disclosing extraterrestrial contact.

The motivations of the disclosure president will likely span several areas. First, the erosion of public trust in institutions may push this leader to embrace transparency, viewing it as a necessary step to restore confidence in the government. In an age when whistleblower testimony and declassified documents are becoming commonplace, this president will understand that secrecy is no longer tenable.

Geopolitics will also play a key role. The United States has always sought to position itself as the global authority, and this would extend to extraterrestrial relations. Just as John F. Kennedy faced pressure during the Cold War to maintain the United States' dominance in space exploration, the disclosure president will strive to ensure that no other nation gains a strategic advantage in the domain of extraterrestrial knowledge and technology.

Ethical considerations may weigh even more heavily. Similar to Bill Clinton's personal efforts to uncover government-held UFO secrets, this leader will likely feel a moral obligation to reveal what's been hidden for decades. The disclosure president will understand that humanity is on the cusp of a seismic shift in its understanding of life in the universe and will feel the responsibility to guide society through this transition—spiritually, socially, and politically.

However, such a decision will not come without internal conflict. The president will have to weigh the possible consequences of disclosure, from societal unrest to economic disruptions, and even spiritual reckonings. Like Richard Nixon, who oversaw an era of government secrecy and the subsequent unraveling of public trust through Watergate, the disclosure president will be walking a tightrope. Yet, with mounting pressure from the public and global allies, this leader will step forward, not only to reveal the truth, but to position humanity for the future.

The President's Address on Historic Extraterrestrial Contact

Although we await an official disclosure announcement, what follows is not *just* a theoretical exercise—it is a glimpse of what *could soon become our reality*, an announcement that will redefine humanity's place in the universe.[105]

My fellow citizens, today marks a turning point not just in American history, but in the history of humanity. After extensive consultation with our national defense, intelligence, and scientific communities, I am here to confirm what has long been suspected: **We are not alone** in this universe.

For the first time, we have undeniable evidence that Earth has been, and continues to be, observed by one or more intelligent, nonhuman entities. This revelation, while extraordinary, has been shared with world leaders across 103 nations, and tonight, many of them are making similar announcements. Together, we have reached the conclusion that the time for secrecy has passed, and the time for transparency is now.

Let me reassure you immediately: There is no indication that we are under attack. All available evidence suggests these visitors are watching, not waging war. Their presence, though profound, appears peaceful. Nevertheless, it is our responsibility to ensure the safety of our nation and the world. In a moment, the Secretary of Defense will outline the immediate steps being taken to secure both our physical and economic security.

To lead our engagement with these new realities, I have signed an Executive Order creating the **Office of Contact Affairs,** which will be housed under the Department of Homeland

Security. This office will work tirelessly to coordinate our response, manage communications with these entities, and provide timely updates to the public. It will report directly to me to ensure complete transparency as we navigate this unprecedented chapter.

Additionally, I have instructed the Attorney General to launch a full investigation into any instances of withheld information regarding these encounters. The public has a right to know, and we will leave no stone unturned in uncovering the truth.

This moment also calls for calm. In order to maintain order and stability, I have authorized the deployment of National Guard resources for any state governor who feels they may be needed. Furthermore, to protect our financial markets during this sensitive time, I am invoking emergency powers to temporarily close the stock market and banking systems for a short period to ensure their stability.

We are entering an era that will challenge much of what we thought we knew. But with challenge comes opportunity. This revelation opens the door to possibilities we could never have imagined—a future wherein humanity may engage with other civilizations and, perhaps, expand our understanding of the cosmos.

We must meet this moment with curiosity, not fear; with hope, not panic. Tonight, we are not just Americans; we are ambassadors of Earth. Together, as a unified world, we will move forward—guided by the principles of peace, cooperation, and shared discovery.

Imminent Disclosure: A Moment on the Horizon

Whoever steps forward as the disclosure president will be doing so at a moment when the tides of secrecy are giving way to the flood of truth, and full transparency is no longer a choice but a necessity. As the evidence mounts, both in this book and across the world, we find ourselves on the edge of an unprecedented moment in human history. The long-with-held truths about extraterrestrial life and our government's knowledge of them are slowly coming to light. While a full disclosure from the president of the United States has not yet been made, the signs indicate that such an announcement is no longer a matter of *if*—but *when*.

History has repeatedly shown us how presidents grapple with secrets of this magnitude. Lyndon B. Johnson presided over the closure of Project Blue Book, the US Air Force's public investigation into UFOs. By ending this official inquiry, Johnson set the precedent for decades of government secrecy, reflecting Cold War policies that shrouded truth behind a veil of confidentiality. Similarly, Ronald Reagan, in his now-famous United Nations speech, hinted at the potential of an alien threat to unify humanity, implying that extraterrestrial realities were contemplated at the highest levels of government. These historical moments, like today, signal the progression toward the inevitable: full disclosure.

Over the decades, governments have maintained secrecy regarding unexplained aerial phenomena, but these barriers are beginning to erode. With each new whistleblower testimony, declassified document, and verified sighting, the veil of mystery lifts further. Even Barack Obama, in recent years, acknowledged the seriousness with which UAPs are being studied, hinting at the weight of evidence building toward disclosure. We are now at a critical juncture, at which the release of such information seems imminent. To fully appreciate where we are, we must first understand the key moments that have brought us here.

The *New York Times* Breakthrough

On December 16, 2017, a bombshell article hit the front page of the *New York Times*, sending shockwaves through the public and the intelligence community. The article, co-written by investigative journalists Leslie Kean, Helene Cooper, and Ralph Blumenthal, was a watershed moment in UFO disclosure. It detailed the existence of the Advanced

Aerospace Threat Identification Program (AATIP), the secretive Pentagon initiative that had been investigating UFOs for years.

Humanity was filled with a mixture of disbelief and intrigue as readers across the globe absorbed the revelations. The article not only confirmed that the US government had been taking UFOs—or UAPs, as they're now known—seriously, but it also revealed the existence of videos that showcased these occurrences in action. Among these videos were the now-famous *Tic Tac*, "*Gimbal*, and *Go Fast* footage, all captured by US Navy pilots.

Leslie Kean's careful documentation and meticulous research gave the article a credibility that couldn't be easily dismissed. The *Times* report wasn't the stuff of tabloid sensationalism—it was grounded in official documents; expert testimonies; and real, verifiable data. For many, this was the moment when the UFO phenomenon moved from the realm of speculation and conspiracy theories into the light of serious inquiry.

AATIP, as the article revealed, had been funded at the behest of then Senate Majority Leader Harry Reid. With a budget of $22 million, AATIP's mission was to investigate reports of UAPs, assess their potential threat to national security, and, if possible, determine their origin.

The article provided a glimpse into the classified world of UAP research, shedding light on cases that had long been kept in the shadows. It was a moment of reckoning—not just for the public, but for the government and military officials who had been tasked with understanding these mysterious phenomena.

As the revelations spread, the world began to grapple with questions that had previously been the domain of science fiction: What are these objects? Where do they come from? And, perhaps most unsettling of all: *What do they want?*

The *Tic Tac*, *Gimbal*, and *Go Fast* Videos

In the wake of the *New York Times* article, the public was introduced to three pieces of video footage that would forever change the conversation about UAPs. The *Tic Tac*, *Gimbal*, and *Go Fast* videos captured by US Navy pilots showcased unidentified aerial phenomena executing maneuvers that defied conventional understanding of aerodynamics and physics.

The *Tic Tac* video, recorded in 2004 by pilots from the USS Nimitz Carrier Strike Group, became the most famous of the three. The footage shows a white, oblong object resembling a Tic Tac breath mint, moving erratically and at incredible speeds. It outmaneuvered the Navy jets that attempted to intercept it, leaving seasoned pilots like Commander David Fravor baffled. "It was moving in ways that no known aircraft can move," Fravor had testified, echoing the sentiments he would later share at the 2023 House Committee hearing.

The *Gimbal* video, recorded in 2015, added further intrigue. It showed an object rotating in midair while flying against strong headwinds—an impossible feat for any known aircraft. The *Go Fast* video, also from 2015, captured an object speeding over the ocean at low altitude, moving so quickly it seemed to defy the very laws of physics.

These videos weren't just anomalies caught on film; they were recorded using some of the most advanced sensors and tracking equipment available, revealing details invisible to the naked eye. The evidence was clear and compelling: Something beyond our current understanding was operating in the skies.

As these videos circulated, they fueled public fascination and governmental scrutiny. The question was no longer whether UAPs existed; the evidence was irrefutable. The question now was, "What are they, and what do they mean for the future of humanity?"

Pentagon Acknowledgment

The release of these videos left the Pentagon with little choice but to officially acknowledge their authenticity. In the days and weeks following the publication, the Pentagon confirmed the authenticity of the videos. This confirmation was more than just an admission; it was a signal to the world that the US government was finally acknowledging the reality of these unidentified aerial phenomena. A once-derided subject was thrust into the mainstream—no longer a topic of whispered speculation, but a matter of national security.

Among those who stepped forward to shed light on these revelations was Luis Elizondo, the former head of the AATIP. His revelations about AATIP's existence and its extensive investigations into UFOs added further weight to the reports. Speaking publicly for the first time, he described the serious and ongoing interest the government had in these phenomena. "These are not just eyewitness accounts," Elizondo stated in interviews. "These are data-driven observations collected through some of the most sophisticated sensors and systems we have."

The Pentagon's acknowledgment and Elizondo's candid discussions ushered in a new era of transparency. What had been hidden in classified reports and secretive programs was now being brought into the light, forcing the public and government officials to confront the undeniable. The implications were staggering—if these objects weren't of human origin, then what were they? And if they were man-made, why did they exhibit capabilities far beyond any known technology?

Formation of the UAP Taskforce

The impact of these revelations reverberated through the highest levels of government, leading to actions that would have been unthinkable just a few years earlier. In 2021, the US Congress held its first hearings on UAPs, a clear indication that the issue was being taken seriously at the highest echelons of power. The testimonies given during these hearings highlighted the urgent need for a comprehensive and transparent approach to studying these phenomena.

In response to mounting public pressure and the need for formal investigation, the Pentagon initiated the formation of the UAP Task Force (UAPTF). This new organization was charged with the responsibility of continuing the work AATIP had started—studying UAP incidents, analyzing data collected, and reporting its findings to Congress on a regular basis. It was a monumental step, reflecting a growing awareness within the government that these encounters could no longer be ignored or dismissed.

The UAPTF wasn't just a bureaucratic formality; it represented a concerted effort to understand what was happening in the skies. The formation of this task force signaled a shift in attitude—a recognition that the potential threat posed by UAPs needed to be thoroughly investigated, not just for the sake of curiosity but for national security.

The public, too, began to pay closer attention. As more information became available, the once-niche subject of UFOs became a topic of serious discussion across the country. What had previously been the domain of enthusiasts and conspiracy theorists was now the focus of official reports and government scrutiny.

Director of National Intelligence Report

Building on the momentum created by the UAP Task Force's investigations, the Office of the Director of National Intelligence compiled its first formal report. In June 2021, the growing interest in UAPs culminated in the release of a landmark report titled *Preliminary Assessment: Unidentified Aerial Phenomena* by the Office of the Director of National Intelligence (ODNI). This report was the result of a comprehensive review of 144 UAP encounters reported by US military personnel between 2004 and 2021. For the first time, the government provided a detailed assessment of these incidents, confirming that UAPs are real and often exhibit flight characteristics that defy conventional explanations.

The report was striking in its frankness. While it didn't confirm the existence of extraterrestrial life, it left open the possibility that some UAPs could have nonhuman origins. The findings were clear: These objects weren't just optical illusions or misidentified weather phenomena. They demonstrated unusual flight characteristics—rapid acceleration, sudden changes in direction, and the ability to operate at extreme altitudes—that couldn't be easily explained by current technology.

The ODNI report also highlighted a critical concern: UAPs posed a potential threat to flight safety. The document emphasized the need for continued investigation and the importance of developing a standardized reporting system for UAP encounters. The acknowledgment that these occurrences could endanger both military and civilian aircraft underscored the urgency of the situation.

The release of this report added unprecedented credibility to the subject of UAPs. No longer was the discussion confined to the fringes of society; it was now a matter of public record, backed by the highest levels of the US government. It fueled public curiosity and concern, leading to widespread debate about the implications of the findings. What did these objects represent? Were they foreign adversaries, or was something even more profound at play?

As the government's acknowledgment of UAPs continued to evolve, one thing became clear: The era of secrecy and dismissal was over. The world was now facing the possibility that humanity might not be alone in the universe, and the implications of that were vast and far-reaching.

Whistleblower Testimony Before Congress in 2023

As the US government's stance on UAPs evolved and more information came to light, it wasn't long before even more explosive revelations emerged in the form of whistleblower testimonies. The year 2023 marked a turning point in the government's approach to unidentified aerial phenomena. The testimonies of former military pilots Ryan Graves and David Fravor, alongside former intelligence officer David Grusch, during the House Committee hearing reverberated far beyond the walls of Washington, DC. While the hearing itself was significant, the aftermath of these testimonies truly highlighted their profound impact on national and global scales.

Graves and Fravor had already shared their harrowing encounters with unknown crafts—vehicles that defied the capabilities of even the most advanced jets in the US arsenal. Their descriptions of objects moving at unimaginable speeds and executing maneuvers that contradicted conventional aeronautics were more than just extraordinary accounts; they were a challenge to the very fabric of what was understood about flight and technology.

As we discovered in the introduction of this book, it was David Grusch's testimony that sent shockwaves through the intelligence and defense communities. As a highly decorated former intelligence officer, his claims about secret US programs dedicated to retrieving and reverse-engineering off-world technology were nothing short of explosive. These "legacy programs," as he described them, had allegedly been in operation for decades, positioning the United States at the forefront of understanding the UFO phenomenon.

Grusch's revelations went beyond the details shared in the hearing. They sparked a wave of interest and concern domestically and internationally, leading to a renewed focus on the potential implications of these findings. His allegations raised critical questions: What exactly has the US government uncovered? How advanced is this off-world technology, and what could it mean for the future of humanity?

The testimonies of Graves, Fravor, and Grusch did more than just inform; they reinforced the view that the United States is leading the global investigation into UAPs. This leadership role is not solely about technological superiority, but also about transparency and disclosure. As these revelations became public and the US House of Representatives and Senate held more hearings, nations around the globe began looking to the US to set the standard for disclosing information about these mysterious objects.

The global reaction was swift. Governments and researchers worldwide started reevaluating their own UAP encounters in light of the US disclosures, fueling a growing demand for transparency and intensifying the international push to reveal what is truly known about these phenomena.

Prominent World Leaders and Their Bombshell Testimonies

Haim Eshed (Former Israeli Space Security Chief)

As these testimonies gained global attention, prominent world leaders began to come forward with their own bombshell disclosures. Haim Eshed, a former Israeli space security chief, made headlines by claiming that extraterrestrial beings exist, and that both the US and Israel have been in contact with them for years. Eshed even suggested former President Donald Trump was on the verge of revealing this information, but was persuaded not to by the extraterrestrial "Galactic Federation," which believed humanity wasn't yet ready for such a revelation.

As the head of Israel's space security programs for three decades, Eshed's credentials lent weight to his claims. According to Eshed, the Galactic Federation had been in communication with the US and Israel, discussing the structure of the universe and sharing advanced technologies.[106] However, these extraterrestrial entities insisted that their existence remain concealed from the general public until humanity was deemed prepared to handle the profound implications of their presence.

Eshed's revelations were reported widely, sparking debates and discussions in the media and scientific communities. While some dismissed his statements as far-fetched, others saw them as a potential breakthrough in the ongoing quest for truth. The idea that world leaders, including a sitting US president, had been privy to such extraordinary information but chose to withhold it from the public raised significant ethical and philosophical questions.

Eshed's claims also highlighted the geopolitical dimensions of the UFO phenomenon. The fact that two major allies, the US and Israel, were allegedly working together on such sensitive matters suggested a coordinated international approach to managing extraterrestrial contact. This collaboration, if true, indicated a level of secrecy and strategic planning that extended beyond national borders.

In addition to Eshed's testimony, other high-profile figures have come forward with their own disclosures.

Rear Admiral Tim Gallaudet (NOAA)

Rear Admiral Tim Gallaudet, a former US Navy officer and oceanographer who led the National Oceanic and Atmospheric Administration (NOAA) under former President Donald Trump, holds a unique position in the study of UAPs and their transmedium capabilities. Gallaudet's background in oceanography and atmospheric science, combined with his military expertise, places him at the forefront of understanding objects that move seamlessly between air and water—unidentified submerged objects (USOs).

NOAA's mission to monitor the Earth's oceans and atmosphere made it a key player in tracking occurrences in these often unexplored realms. Under Gallaudet's leadership, the agency oversaw advanced radar, sonar, and satellite technologies—tools that could detect and analyze UAPs and USOs. This capability is essential, as many UAP sightings, including the infamous 2004 "Tic Tac" incident, occurred near vast bodies of water like the Pacific Ocean. That object's transition from air to water without losing velocity illustrates the mysterious transmedium capabilities of these crafts, baffling experts in propulsion and physics.

Gallaudet's tenure at NOAA under Trump highlights the importance of combining scientific exploration with national security concerns. His support for UAP whistleblower David Grusch's claims of a secret UFO retrieval program demonstrates his belief that the study of these phenomena requires serious attention from the military and scientific communities. The collaboration between NOAA's scientific resources and the Pentagon's defense priorities under the Trump administration paved the way for a broader approach to UFO investigations.

His expertise not only bridges the gap between atmospheric and oceanic phenomena, but also reinforces the need for an interdisciplinary approach to understanding these elusive objects. Gallaudet's insights are critical in expanding the scope of UAP studies to include our planet's oceans, potentially revealing hidden pathways or bases for these unidentified crafts. His work continues to push the boundaries of scientific inquiry and national security, solidifying his role as a key figure in UAP and USO research.

Retired US Army Colonel Karl Nell

Retired US Army Colonel Karl Nell has taken the conversation on extraterrestrial encounters a step further, boldly claiming that aliens not only exist, but are actively interacting with humans. His statements, made at the 2024 SALT Conference, have added considerable weight to the growing body of credible testimonies supporting the reality of extraterrestrial engagement.

As the former director of the Pentagon's UAP task force, Nell's background lends undeniable authority to his assertions. His involvement in the highest levels of US military intelligence offers rare insight into classified investigations concerning unidentified aerial phenomena. Nell has emphasized that these interactions aren't just fringe concerns—they represent a key aspect of national security and scientific inquiry.

Nell's statements go beyond curiosity and speculation, bringing the potential geopolitical ramifications into sharp focus. As the former UAP task force director, he saw firsthand how these phenomena could challenge airspace sovereignty, global defense protocols, and technological advancements. According to Nell, recognizing and addressing alien interactions is essential for scientific discovery and protecting national interests.

His claims have sparked renewed interest in governmental disclosure, as well as raised questions about the extent of military knowledge concerning extraterrestrial encounters. With mounting evidence from whistleblowers, defense experts, and former officials, Nell's perspective challenges governments to approach the UFO occurrences not just as anomalies, but as a pressing national and global security issue.

Colonel Nell's stance marks a critical juncture in the ongoing debate over UAPs and extraterrestrial life. His credentials and authority in military intelligence elevate his testimony beyond typical UFO claims, making his voice hard to dismiss in the evolving narrative on UFOs, government secrecy, and potential alien interactions.

Senate Majority Leader Chuck Schumer

In a significant legislative move, Senate Majority Leader Chuck Schumer proposed an amendment aimed at increasing transparency regarding

UAPs. The amendment includes language about nonhuman intelligence and seeks to declassify government documents related to UFOs. Schumer's initiative reflects a broader push within the government to acknowledge and investigate the UFO phenomenon openly. This legislative effort is part of a growing recognition that the public has a right to know about the activities and findings related to UAPs.

The Schumer amendment represents a critical step toward demystifying the government's involvement with UFOs. By mandating the declassification of documents and promoting transparency, this legislation aims to build public trust and foster a more informed discourse on the subject. Schumer's comments highlight the need for accountability and openness, emphasizing that understanding UAPs is not just a matter of national security, but also of scientific curiosity and public interest.

James Lacatski, Retired Defense Intelligence Agency (DIA) Intelligence Officer

At the conclusion of a 2011 meeting in the Capitol building with a US senator and an agency under secretary, James Lacatski made a shocking revelation, which he later documented in chapter 9 of his eye-opening 2023 book, *Inside the US Government Covert UFO Program: Initial Revelations.*

> He stated that the United States was in possession of a craft of unknown origin and had successfully gained access to its interior. This craft had a streamlined configuration suitable for aerodynamic flight but no intakes, exhaust, wings, or control surfaces. In fact, it appeared not to have an engine, fuel tanks, or fuel. Lacatski asked: What was the purpose of this craft? Was it a life-support craft useful only for atmospheric reentry or what? If it was a spacecraft, then how did it operate?[107]

Lacatski is known for his involvement in the US government's investigation into UAPs. He played a key role in the Advanced Aerospace Weapon System Applications Program (AAWSAP), a secretive Pentagon program initiated in 2007 to study anomalous aerial phenomena and potential aerospace threats. This program is closely related to the later, more widely known AATIP, which gained public attention through media reports in 2017. Lacatski's work was part of a broader effort to assess the implications of UAP sightings on national security, as well as to investigate advanced propulsion technologies and other scientific anomalies. He collaborated with a range of experts, including scientists, defense contractors, and intelligence officers, to explore the possibilities of unknown technologies.

Lacatski's contributions, while not widely publicized, have been crucial in shaping the modern governmental approach to UAP research and have fueled ongoing debates about extraterrestrial life, advanced technologies, and the extent of government knowledge on the subject. His revelation that the United States was in possession of a craft of unknown origin, with full access to its interior, stands as a landmark moment in UAP disclosure. This stunning omission not only challenges conventional understanding, but raises profound questions about humanity's place in the universe and what hidden technological and extraterrestrial discoveries may still lie ahead.

Renewed Scientific Interest

Avi Loeb, Professor of Science at Harvard University

There is a shift towards serious academic inquiry into the UFO phenomenon. Avi Loeb is an Israeli-American theoretical physicist and astronomer known for his pioneering work in astrophysics, cosmology, and extraterrestrial intelligence. He is a professor of science at Harvard University, where he has served as the chair of the Department of Astronomy. Loeb has made significant contributions to the study of black holes, the first stars, the search for extraterrestrial life, and the study of exoplanets.

Loeb gained widespread attention in recent years for his hypothesis that the interstellar object 'Oumuamua, discovered in 2017, could be a potential alien artifact or probe. He proposed that the object's unusual characteristics—its acceleration, shape, and lack of a visible cometary tail—suggested it might not be a natural asteroid or comet, but rather a piece of advanced technology from an extraterrestrial civilization. This idea was highly controversial, but sparked renewed interest in the scientific search for extraterrestrial life.

In 2021, Loeb published a book titled *Extraterrestrial: The First Sign of Intelligent Life Beyond Earth*, in which he outlined his views on 'Oumuamua and called for a serious scientific investigation into the possibility of intelligent extraterrestrial life. He also leads the Galileo Project, an initiative aimed at systematically searching for evidence of extraterrestrial technology, including unidentified aerial phenomena.

In 2023, Loeb led an expedition to the crash site to recover fragments of the object from the ocean floor. The mission aimed to collect and analyze these fragments to determine their composition and potential extraterrestrial origin. Preliminary findings from this expedition have sparked considerable interest, as the recovered materials exhibited unusual properties that may not align with known terrestrial or meteoritic compositions.

These efforts highlight Loeb's commitment to empirical evidence and his willingness to explore unconventional avenues of scientific inquiry. By conducting systematic searches and rigorous analyses of such materials, Loeb is not only advancing the field of UAP research, but also challenging the scientific community to consider the possibility of extraterrestrial technology.

Gary Nolan, Respected Scientist and Professor of Pathology at Stanford University

Gary Nolan brings substantial credibility to the study of UFOs and UAPs. Known for his pioneering work in immunology and cancer research, Nolan's involvement in the UAP field has garnered significant attention and respect. His research primarily focuses on the biological and neurological impacts of UAP encounters, investigating how they might affect human health and consciousness. Nolan has conducted studies on individuals who have had close encounters, examining potential physio-logical changes and anomalies. His rigorous scientific approach and use of advanced technologies lend a level of legitimacy and seriousness to the field, encouraging other scientists to approach the topic with the same level of scholarly precision and open-minded inquiry.

The History of Government Programs and UFOs

While recent UFO events have captured significant attention, the gov-ernment's interest in unidentified aerial phenomena is not new; it has a long and intricate history. The declassification of programs like KONA BLUE has further illuminated the extent of government involvement in UFO research. KONA BLUE, a DHS special-access program termi-nated in 2012, was intended to be a classified research initiative related to recovered UAPs, but it never fully materialized. The release of recent documents associated with this program has provided valuable insights into the seriousness with which the government approaches the subject.

What is truly striking is the realization that the phenomenon has been studied worldwide for decades. The following chart is compre-hensive list of known government UFO programs across the globe. It highlights the collective effort to decode its mysteries.

Country	Program	Years Active	Leadership
United States	Project Sign	1948–1949	General Nathan Twining, Colonel Howard McCoy
United States	Project Grudge	1949–1951	Colonel Harold Watson, Captain Edward Ruppelt
United States	Project Blue Book	1952–1969	Captain Edward J. Ruppelt, Dr. J. Allen Hynek (consultant)

Country	Program	Years Active	Leadership
United States	Advanced Aerospace Weapon System Applications Program (AAWSAP)	2007–2012	Dr. James Lacatski
United States	Advanced Aerospace Threat Identification Program (AATIP)	2007–2012	Luis Elizondo
United States	Unidentified Aerial Phenomena Task Force (UAPTF)	2020–2021	U.S. Navy personnel (specific leadership not widely publicized)
United States	All-domain Anomaly Resolution Office (AARO)	2022–Present	Director Sean Kirkpatrick (current)
Chile	Committee for the Study of Anomalous Aerial Phenomena (CEFAA)	1997–Present	General Ricardo Bermúdez (initial director)
France	Groupe d'Études et d'Informations sur les Phénomènes Aérospatiaux Non-identifiés (GEIPAN)	1977–Present	Claude Poher (founder), Xavier Passot (director until recently)
United Kingdom	Flying Saucer Working Party (FSWP)	1950–1951	Sir Henry Tizard
United Kingdom	Ministry of Defence UFO Desk	1950–2009	Nick Pope (1991-1994 during his tenure)
Canada	Project Magnet	1950–1954	Wilbert Smith
Canada	Project Second Storey	1952–1954	Defense Research Board (specific leaders not well-documented)
Brazil	Sistema de Investigação de Objetos Aéreos Não Identificados (SIOANI)	1969–1972	Colonel João Adil Oliveira

Country	Program	Years Active	Leadership
Soviet Union/ Russia	Setka	1978–1990s	Colonel Boris Sokolov, Academician Vasily Kaznacheev
Argentina	Comisión de Estudio de Fenómenos Aeroespaciales (CEFAE)	2011– Present	Commodore Guillermo Daniel Miguel
Japan	Unidentified Aerial Phenomena Clarification League for Security-Oriented National Security	2024– Present	Formed in 2024 (Leadership not yet fully documented)

The journey from skepticism to serious inquiry into UFOs and UAPs has been long and fraught with challenges. For years, the subject was relegated to the realm of conspiracy theories, often dismissed with a mocking reference to "tinfoil hats." However, one thing is certain: The UFO phenomenon is no longer confined to the fringes of society; it's now a subject of rigorous investigation and global importance.

Surveying the long history of the UFO demands this question: Are all these programs studying something that doesn't exist? The sheer number of government initiatives, spanning multiple decades and numerous countries, screams, "No!" These programs involve highly trained military personnel, scientists, and intelligence officers dedicating substantial resources and time to investigating unexplained aerial phenomena.

The consistent effort and serious inquiry into these sightings suggest there is indeed something substantial at play. This isn't just about speculative fiction or the wild imaginations of conspiracy theorists. Instead, it indicates a pattern of examining something real. From the US Project Sign in 1948 to the more recent efforts by Japan's Unidentified Aerial Phenomena Clarification League established in 2024, the global commitment to understanding these events underscores their significance.

Why would so many credible institutions and experts fund these studies if there were truly nothing to discover?

Looking Ahead

As we prepare to hear the Founding Fathers' final message, a critical question arises: How do the principles of the Founders, who were deeply rooted in their faith, speak to the spiritual and theological challenges of today?

The possibility of extraterrestrial life isn't just a matter of political transparency—it's a test of spiritual resilience. For the Church, this moment calls for more than defending our beliefs; it requires grappling with revelations that could reshape our understanding of the cosmos and God's role within it.

In our last chapter, we will confront the tension between the Founders' message and the impending disclosure. What does it mean to uphold the Liberty Code when the very fabric of creation is questioned? How do we, as believers, stand firm against a deception threatening to undermine the foundations of our faith? As we uncover the deeper layers of the Founders' faith, we'll discover how their legacy provides a roadmap for navigating these profound revelations.

Chapter 14

THE FOUNDERS' FINAL MESSAGE

> The God who gave us life, gave us liberty at the same time;
> the hand of force may destroy, but cannot disjoin them.
>
> —THOMAS JEFFERSON

We began our journey in 1796 at the First Presbyterian Church on High Street at noon. It was here in Philadelphia that the Founding Fathers—President George Washington, members of Congress, and esteemed dignitaries—honored their fallen patriot, David Rittenhouse, while thoughtfully contemplating the possibility of beings from other worlds. We have come full circle, as our nation's leaders gather once again, over two centuries later, to confront this same reality.

Whether some claim the visitors are extraterrestrial or, as I believe, spiritual entities (i.e., demons and fallen angels) from other realms, one truth remains: Christ is Lord over all creation. As Colossians 1:16 declares:

> For by him all things were created in the heavens and on the earth, visible things and invisible things, whether thrones or dominions or principalities or powers. All things have been created through him and for him." (Colossians 1:16, WEB)

No matter what may come, Christ's reign gives us hope, strength, and confidence to stand firm.

Just as the Founding Fathers relied on God's direction as they faced the unknown challenges of their time, so, too, we must now, as we confront disclosure. Their belief in divine sovereignty, which guided the birth of this nation, must now lead us as we navigate this unprecedented crisis.

The Founding Fathers, in their contemplation of the cosmos and Christ's sovereignty over all creation, weren't only concerned with philosophical reflections; they faced practical and immediate challenges in shaping a new nation. As they grappled with questions of governance, it became clear that the ideals they embraced would be tested by the harsh realities of forming a unified government.

This tension came to a head during the 1787 Constitutional Convention, where the fate of the fledgling nation hung in the balance. As the delegates gathered in the oppressive Philadelphia heat, they found themselves gridlocked over the nation's future. The debate over representation seemed endless, with each side unyielding. Should states be represented equally, or should population determine their power? Weeks of fierce arguments and countless proposals had failed to yield a solution. The atmosphere grew dire, with some delegates feeling the very fate of America hung by a thread.

An air of desperation thickened in Independence Hall. The prospect of failure weighed heavily on the delegates, as the idea of a fractured union began to seem more likely than the establishment of a lasting government. It was against this backdrop of looming collapse on June 28, 1787, that Benjamin Franklin, the eldest and most respected statesman among them, rose to speak. All eyes turned to him as he addressed George Washington, who presided in silence over the assembly.

"MR. PRESIDENT," Franklin began, the men in the chamber stilling at the sound of his voice. His words, though measured, carried the gravity of a person who had lived long enough to understand both the weight of history and the peril of the moment.

The small Progress we have made, after 4 or 5 weeks' close Atten-
dance and continual Reasonings with each other, our different
Sentiments on almost every Question, several of the last producing as many Noes as Ayes, is, methinks, a melancholy Proof of
the Imperfection of the Human Understanding. We indeed seem
to feel our own want of political Wisdom, since we have been
running all about in Search of it. We have gone back to ancient
History for Models of Government, and examined the different
Forms of those Republics, which, having been originally formed
with the Seeds of their own Dissolution, now no longer exist;
and we have viewed modern States all round Europe, but find
none of their Constitutions suitable to our circumstances.[108]

Franklin's admission of their struggle resonated deeply with the
assembly. In that tense moment, it was as though the heaviness of history bore down upon them. He spoke not only to their frustrations but
to the broader human experience of reaching for solutions and finding
only dead ends.

In this Situation of this Assembly, groping, as it were, in the dark
to find Political Truth, and scarce able to distinguish it when
presented to us, how has it happened, Sir, that we have not hith-
erto once thought of humbly applying to the Father of Lights to
illuminate our Understandings?[109]

He continued:

In the Beginning of the Contest with Britain, when we were
sensible of Danger, we had daily Prayers in this Room for the
Divine Protection. Our Prayers, Sir, were heard;—and they were
graciously answered. All of us, who were engaged in the Struggle, must have observed frequent Instances of a superintending
Providence in our Favor.[110]

His words struck a chord, calling the delegates to remember how Providence had seemingly guided them through the darkest days of the Revolution. Now, Franklin urged, was no time to abandon that source of strength:

> To that kind Providence we owe this happy Opportunity of Consulting in Peace on the Means of establishing our future national Felicity. And have we now forgotten that powerful Friend? Or do we imagine we no longer need its assistance? I have lived, Sir, a long time; and the longer I live, the more convincing proofs I see of this Truth, that GOD governs in the Affairs of Men. And if a Sparrow cannot fall to the Ground without his Notice, is it probable that an Empire can rise without his Aid?[111]

In this humble yet powerful appeal, Franklin drove home the point that their efforts would be no better than the builders of Babel without divine guidance, warning, "And, what is worse, Mankind may hereafter, from this unfortunate Instance, despair of establishing Government by human Wisdom, and leave it to Chance, War, and Conquest."[112]

Franklin concluded with a motion that, from then on, the assembly would begin each day with prayer, seeking Heaven's assistance. His call wasn't only a plea for unity, but a recognition that their endeavor was, at its heart, a spiritual quest as much as a political one.

Two years later, on April 30, 1789, echoing this sentiment, George Washington, in his inaugural address, expressed the profound need for divine guidance to navigate their present crisis:

> No people can be bound to acknowledge and adore the Invisible Hand which conducts the affairs of men more than those of the United States. Every step by which they have advanced to the character of an independent nation seems to have been distinguished by some token of providential agency; and in the important revolution just accomplished in the system of their

united government the tranquil deliberations and voluntary consent of so many distinct communities from which the event has resulted can not be compared with the means by which most governments have been established without some return of pious gratitude, along with an humble anticipation of the future blessings which the past seem to presage. These reflections, arising out of the present crisis, have forced themselves too strongly on my mind to be suppressed.[113]

As we reflect on his words, we must recognize that our current situation demands the same reliance on God's providence as we confront a cosmic crisis that threatens to reshape our understanding of humanity's place in the universe.

The Liberty Code

As we stand on the threshold of a monumental shift in human history—one with which the reality of extraterrestrial life may soon be disclosed—the Church finds itself at a critical juncture. How will we, as the Body of Christ, respond? For too long, the topic of UFOs and extraterrestrial intelligence has been dismissed or relegated to fringe conversations. But what if tomorrow brings confirmation? This isn't simply an intellectual exercise—it is a spiritual imperative. Disclosure is not just a revelation—it's a reckoning.

As we consider the spiritual implications of disclosure, we must anchor ourselves in what I call the "Liberty Code": the belief that true freedom—both spiritual and physical—is found only through reliance on God's guiding hand. The Founding Fathers understood this when they built the foundation of this nation—not just in politics, but in faith, trusting in what President Washington described as "God's invisible hand."

If we're not prepared to hold fast to this truth, our faith could falter, our communities could fracture, and the Church may lose its voice in one of the most significant moments of our time. Imagine the shock-wave of doubt and confusion that will ripple through congregations if we crumble at the disclosure. For many, it would feel like a spiritual earthquake, shaking the very foundations of their belief in God's sovereignty. Some may mistake extraterrestrial beings for spiritual guides or cosmic gods, leading them into deception that draws them away from Christ. Many will question how God fits into a universe that includes outer-space beings.

If we are unprepared or stay silent, we risk losing the next generation to darkness.

We must be a beacon of hope and clarity, not another voice of uncertainty. Undoubtedly, many will have questions, and some may feel isolated in their confusion. Churches must foster environments where congregants can safely ask questions, wrestle with doubts, and explore how these new revelations fit within their faith. Small groups and Bible studies should be equipped to guide these conversations with grace and truth. In these times, the Liberty Code must guide us.

As Abraham Lincoln reminded a fledgling nation, "Our reliance is not in armies; it is in the love of liberty which God has planted in our hearts."[114] May our country, communities, and churches heed the wisdom of America's Founding Fathers, who understood that true freedom is not found in the power of muskets, but in the all-powerful God. That is the essence of Liberty—the freedom they desired for all. In the words of William Lloyd Garrison (1805–1879), "Liberty for each, Liberty for all, Liberty forever!"

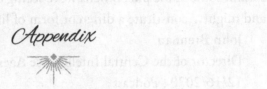

Appendix

UFO QUOTES

In recent years, a growing body of testimonies from high-ranking officials, military personnel, and intelligence agencies has brought unidentified aerial phenomena into the spotlight. Many of the following statements, sourced from individuals with decades of experience in government and defense, confirm that UAPs are being observed with increasing frequency, yet remain largely unexplained. These revelations, compiled from *UAP Guide* (https://www.uap.guide), present a compelling case for further investigation into what these objects are and what they could mean for national security and our understanding of the world.

The following section contains a series of quotes from respected sources, all of whom have acknowledged the reality of UAPs. Their testimonies underscore the urgency and importance of the UAP discussion, pointing to the need for transparency, scientific inquiry, and serious consideration of the implications these phenomena pose.

We have things flying over our military bases and places where we're conducting military exercises, and we don't know what it is, and it isn't ours.

Marco Rubio
US senator (R)
7/16/2020 | Fox News

I think some of the phenomena we're seeing continues to be unexplained and might…constitute a different form of life.

John Brennan
Director of the Central Intelligence Agency
12/16/2020 | Podcast

Usually we have multiple sensors picking up these things…. There are a lot more sightings than have been made public…objects that have been seen by Navy or Air Force pilots, or in satellite imagery, that engage in actions that…we don't have the technology for, or traveling at speeds that exceed the sound barrier without a sonic boom…technologies that we don't have and, frankly, that we are not capable of defending against.

John Ratcliffe
Director of National Intelligence
3/22/2021 | Fox News

So it's not us, that's one thing we know. I could say that with very high degree of confidence in part because of the positions I held in the department.

Christopher Mellon
Deputy assistant secretary of defense for Intelligence
5/16/2021 | 60 Minutes

There is footage and records of objects in the skies. We don't know exactly what they are. We can't explain how they moved, their trajectory. They did not have an easily explainable pattern.

Barack Obama
US president (D)
5/19/2021 | Late Late Show with James Corden

I don't know what it is, but any time you have legitimate pilots describing something that doesn't seem to conform to the laws of physics that govern aviation and is in US airspace, I think it's something we need to get to the bottom of.... If there is a foreign government that had these kinds of capabilities, I think we would see other indications of advanced technology. I can't imagine that what has been described or shown in some of the videos belongs to any government that I'm aware of.... I have no idea what it is but I think we should figure it out.

Martin Heinrich
US senator (D)
5/21/21 | TMZ

There are things flying around out there that we haven't fully identified yet.

Bill Clinton
US president (D)
6/8/2021 | Live with Kelly and Mark

That leaves aliens, which we presume it probably is, although I don't wanna go too far here.

Ben Rhodes
Deputy National Security adviser
6/30/2021 | Podcast

We were able to identify one reported UAP with high confidence. In that case, we identified the object as a large, deflating balloon. The other [143] remain unexplained.... Most of the UAP reported probably do represent physical objects given that a majority of UAP were registered across multiple sensors, to include radar, infrared, electro-optical, weapon seekers, and visual observation. We currently lack data to indicate any UAP are part of a foreign collection program or indicative of a major technological advancement by a potential adversary.... Some UAP observations could be attributable to developments and classified programs by U.S. entities. We were unable to confirm, however, that these systems accounted for any of the [144] UAP reports we collected.

Office of the Director of National Intelligence
Preliminary Assessment: Unidentified Aerial Phenomena 2021
6/25/2021 | Report to Congress

Well. I don't believe they are coming from foreign adversaries. Why, if there were, that would suggest they have a technology that is in a whole different sphere than anything we understand—and, frankly, China and Russia just aren't there, and neither are we by the way.

Mitt Romney
US senator (R), former presidential nominee
6/27/2021 | CNN

We hope it's not an adversary here on Earth that has that kind of technology. But it's something.

Bill Nelson
NASA administrator
10/19/2021 | UVA Center for Politics

There's always the question of "is there something else that we simply do not understand, that might come extraterrestrially?"

Avril Haines
Director of National Intelligence
11/16/2021 | Washington Post

It's clear that the majority, that many of the observations that we have are physical objects from the sensor data…. We haven't had a collision. We have had at least 11 near misses.

Scott Bray
Deputy director of Navy Intelligence
5/17/2022 | Congressional hearings

There are so many of us now on the intel committee and armed services that we're going to stand by the service members who documented this stuff. They have video. They have radar. They have heat sensors. They have everything.

Kirsten Gillibrand
US senator (D), Committee on Armed Services
8/26/2022 | Twitter

UAP continue to represent a hazard to flight safety and pose a possible adversary collection threat. Since the publication of the ODNI preliminary assessment in June 2021, UAP reporting has increased, partially due to a concentrated effort to destigmatize the topic of UAP and instead recognize the potential risks that it poses as both a safety of flight hazard and potential adversarial activity. Whereas there were previously 144 UAP reports covered during the 17 years of UAP reporting included in the ODNI preliminary assessment on UAP, there have been 247 more UAP reports during the 17 months since.

Office of the Director of National Intelligence
2022 Annual Report on Unidentified Aerial Phenomena
1/12/2023 | Report to Congress

The American public can reasonably expect to get some answers to questions that have been burning in the minds of millions of Americans for many years. If nothing else, this [legislation] should either clear up something that's been a cloud hanging over the Air Force and Department of Defense for decades, or it might lead in another direction, which could be truly incredible. There's a lot at stake.

Christopher Mellon
Deputy assistant secretary of defense for Intelligence
1/13/23 | The New York Times

What are UAP, and why are we hearing more about them? I passed legislation requiring more reporting and analysis of unidentified sightings. Now we have much more data about balloons, drones, and other aerial phenomena so we can better protect our skies. This congressionally-mandated report released last month highlights why it's so important to reduce stigma for reporting unidentified sightings, and why AARO [All-domain Anomaly Resolution Office], the office I helped create, is protecting our safety by rigorously investigating those reports.

Kirsten Gillibrand
US senator (D), Committee on Armed Services
2/13/2023 | Twitter

Advanced objects demonstrating advanced technology are routinely flying over our restricted or sensitive airspace posing a risk to both flight safety & national security.

Marco Rubio
US senator (R)
2/28/2023 | Twitter

In the coming days, I will launch Americans for Safe Aerospace (ASA), a new advocacy organization for aerospace safety and national security. ASA will support pilots and other aerospace professionals who are reporting UAP. Our goal is to demand more disclosure from our public officials about this significant safety and national security problem.... If the phenomena I witnessed with my own eyes turns out to be foreign drones, they pose an urgent threat to national security and airspace safety. If they are something else, it must be a scientific priority to find out.

Ryan Graves
Founder, Americans for Safe Aerospace, former F/A-18 pilot
2/28/2023 | Politico

We see these ["metallic orbs"] all over the world, and we see these making very interesting apparent maneuvers.

Dr. Sean Kirkpatrick
Director, All-domain Anomaly Resolution Office
5/31/2023 | NASA IST Briefing

The [UAP Disclosure Act of 2023] introduced as an amendment to the National Defense Authorization Act (NDAA) that will be on the Senate floor next week, would direct the National Archives and Records Administration (NARA) to create a collection of records to be known as the UAP Records Collection and direct every government office to identify which records would fall into the collection. The UAP Records Collection would carry the presumption of immediate disclosure, which means that a review board would have to provide a reasoning for the documents to stay classified.... Former Majority Leader Harry Reid sponsored a project to investigate incidents surrounding UAPs. After that project became public, Senators, Congressmen, committees, and staff began to pursue this issue and uncovered a vast web of individuals and groups with ideas and stories to share. While these stories have varying levels of credibility, the sheer number and variety has led some in Congress to believe that the Executive Branch was concealing important information regarding UAPs over broad periods of time. Congress recognizes that these records—if they exist—were likely concealed under the good faith goal of protecting national security. However, hiding that information from both Congress and the public at large is simply unacceptable. Our goal is to work cooperatively with the executive branch to responsibly disclose these documents and bring the topic into the public sphere in a process that the American people can trust.

US Senate
Joint bipartisan statement from Senators Schumer, Rounds, Rubio, Gillibrand, Young and Heinrich
7/14/2023 | Press Release

For decades, many Americans have been fascinated by objects mysterious and unexplained and it's long past time they get some answers. The American public has a right to learn about technologies of unknown origins, non-human intelligence, and unexplainable phenomena. We are not only working to declassify what the government has previously learned about these phenomena but to create a pipeline for future research to be made public. I am honored to carry on the legacy of my mentor and dear friend, Harry Reid, and fight for the transparency that the public has long demanded surround these unexplained phenomena.

Chuck Schumer
US senator (D), Senate majority leader
7/14/2023 | Press Release

A number of these [whistleblowers] believe and have stated—and we believe them now—that they have seen something. And we are investigating.

Dr. Sean Kirkpatrick
Director, All-domain Anomaly Resolution Office
7/20/2023 | ABC News

I can tell you that advanced UAP are a national security and an aviation safety problem. It has been more than a decade since my squadron began witnessing advanced UAP demonstrating complex maneuvers on a regular basis, and we still don't have answers. I founded Americans for Safe Aerospace to create a center of support, research, and public education for aircrew impacted by UAP encounters.... Today, I would like to center our discussion around three critical issues that demand our immediate attention and concerted action.... As we convene here, UAP are in our airspace, but they are grossly underreported.... The stigma attached to UAP is real and powerful and challenges national security.... The government knows more about UAP than shared publicly, and excessive classification practices keep crucial information hidden.

Ryan Graves
Founder, Americans for Safe Aerospace, former F/A-18 pilot
7/26/23 | Testimony to Congress

In 2019, the UAPTF director tasked me to identify all Special Access Programs & Controlled Access Programs (SAPs/CAPs) we needed to satisfy our congressionally mandated mission. At the time, due to my extensive executive-level intelligence support duties, I was cleared to literally all relevant compartments and in a position of extreme trust in both my military and civilian capacities. I was informed, in the course of my official duties, of a multi decade UAP crash retrieval and reverse engineering program to which I was denied access to those additional read-ons. I made the decision based on the data I collected, to report this information to my superiors and multiple Inspectors General, and in effect become a whistleblower.

David Grusch
National Geospatial Intelligence Agency officer
7/26/23 | Testimony to Congress

There is a lot of unidentified aerial phenomena out there. That's true. And they've got pilot reports, there's various other sensors out there, and some of it is difficult to explain…some [UAPs are] really kind of weird and unexplainable

General Mark Milley
Chairman of the Joint Chiefs of Staff
8/6/2023 | *Washington Times*

We've also been notified by multiple credible sources that information on UAPs has also been withheld from Congress, which if true, is a violation of laws requiring full notification to the legislative branch…. It is an outrage the House didn't work with us on our UAP proposal for a review board. This means declassification of UAP records will be up to the same entities that have blocked and obfuscated their disclosure for decades. We will keep working to change the status quo.

Chuck Schumer
US senator (D), Senate majority leader
12/13/2023 | Senate floor speech

I have met with pilots…they are not conspiratorial, they are not crazy, and they tell me stories that they've seen things that you wouldn't believe. Am I a believer? No, I can't say I am. But I have met with people, serious people, that say there are some really strange things flying around out there.

Donald Trump
US president (R)
6/14/2024 | Podcast

[Congressional staffer]: Can you provide us a specific example of an object that can't be explained as having been human made or natural?

[Bray]: I mean the example that I would say is still unresolved, that I think everyone understands quite well is the 2004 incident from [the USS] Nimitz [aircraft carrier]. We have data on that, and it simply remains unresolved...

Scott Bray
Deputy director of Navy Intelligence
5/17/2022 | Congressional hearings

The most compelling case is the [USS] Nimitz case. Because you have so many witnesses and so many sensors and the FLIR [video] is part of that, but you have to look at the whole case. You have to talk to all the pilots involved [Commander Fravor and Lieutenant Dietrich and their backseat Weapons Systems Officers], which I have done. You have to talk to the radar operators on the [USS] Princeton [Kevin Day and Gary Voorhis]. There's also radar operators up on the E2C Hawkeye which was up there monitoring this.... Then you have this third F/A-18 [pilot Lt. Underwood] that goes up and takes that [FLIR] video. So there is a lot of different information from a lot of different sources and the thing is, it is all perfectly congruent. It all hangs together. No one is contradicting someone else's story. And what people are seeing is what the sensors are reporting. So that case overall is the most compelling to my mind.

Christopher Mellon
Deputy assistant secretary of defense for Intelligence
5/30/2021 | The Joe Rogan Experience

We were off the coast of San Diego; USS Nimitz carrier strike group was getting ready to go on deployment. At around the evening of the tenth of November 2004, all these contacts were popping up on my radar coverage right off Catalina Island right by Los Angeles. At first there were ten or twelve objects. Watching them on the display was like watching snow fall from the sky. Their relative position didn't change from each other moving real slow, 28,000 feet at 100 knots, which is extremely weird. Usually things that high don't travel that slowly because they'll fall out of the sky.

Kevin Day
Senior chief, US Navy; lead radar operator, *USS Princeton*
2021 | Unidentified S1 Ep 2: Raining UFOs

The SPY [radar] guys came down and said "Oh we got clutter".... Asked me to reset all the computer systems. Brought it all back up and lo and behold, they're there still. Then we started getting confirmation from the other ships that they were seeing it too. We were just seeing three tracks. Sometimes they were only going a couple hundred knots, sometimes they were stationary, sometimes they were going really fast. The way they went around us, it looked like they were just monitoring us.

Gary Voorhis
Petty officer, US Navy; radar technician, *USS Princeton*
2019 | Unidentified S1 Ep 2: Raining UFOs

[The Aegis SPY-1 radar] eliminated the possibility that it could have been friendly aircraft of some kind, enemy aircraft of some kind. Nothing really fit.... I was just chomping at the bit. I really wanted to intercept these things.... All of a sudden, this object drops 28,000 feet down to the surface, and I figured it out later, it was 0.78 seconds. [24,000 miles per hour, more than 30 times the speed of sound]. Captain said, "OK, let's go intercept one," and I said, "Hell yeah."

Kevin Day
Senior chief, US Navy; lead radar operator, *USS Princeton*
2021 | Unidentified S1 Ep 2: Raining UFOs

We were operating off the coast of California in a designated working area with our carrier strike group. We had launched to perform a practice flight against each other. Clear blue skies, middle of the day. We were interrupted by a ship born controller. The tone was urgent. Their requests were unusual. "This is not an exercise; this is a real world intercept."

Alex Dietrich
Lieutenant, US Navy; F/A-18 pilot
2019 | Unidentified S1 Ep 1: The UFO Insiders

We grabbed one of the flights that was doing a check flight off the carrier. It happened to be Commander Fravor's flight. They got into an area which we call merge plot, where the pilot is in the visual arena with whatever they are intercepting.

Kevin Day
Senior chief, US Navy; lead radar operator, *USS Princeton*
2021 | Unidentified S1 Ep 2: Raining UFOs

There was something in the water…. There was churning…. We were all clamoring to get on the radio. "Do you see, in the water, what the f* is that?" No windows. No flight surfaces. Smooth. White. No intakes. No smoke trails. It looked like a giant Tic Tac. Maybe 40 feet. Large enough to scare the crap out of me. It was so unnerving because it was so unpredictable. High *g* [-force turns], rapid velocity, rapid acceleration, so you're thinking "How can I possibly fight this?"… [Commander Fravor] had that fighting instinct, so it wasn't surprising his actions on that day. This object seemed to recognize that we were there and went from low altitude to maneuvering in an erratic very rapid manner. The hair on the back of my neck is standing up. I am thinking, *I am going to be watching a disaster*.

Alex Dietrich
Lieutenant, US Navy; F/A-18 pilot
2019 | Unidentified S1 Ep 1: The UFO Insiders

I wanted to see what it was. If I could have joined right up on it and gotten Blue Angel close, then I probably would have done that.

David Fravor
Commander, US Navy; F/A-18 pilot and Black Aces squadron commander
2019 | Unidentified S1 Ep 1: The UFO Insiders

It's about 40 feet long. It's white. It has no wings. It has no rotors. It has no control surfaces. Think of a white Tic Tac.

David Fravor

Commander, US Navy; F/A-18 pilot and Black Aces squadron commander

2019 | Unidentified S1 Ep 2: Raining UFOs

This thing would go instantaneous from one way to another similar to if you threw a ping-pong ball against a wall. And we start to kind of orbit, because we are going to watch this thing…. It is still doing its erratic thing around this disturbance in the water, and I say "Hey, I am going to go check it out, I am going to go down there"…. And, all of a sudden, it goes [zip] and it kind of turns, now it's mirroring us, it seems to know we are here…. It goes from almost a hover to a pretty aggressive climb up to our altitude. So now there is a bit of fear, because you have no idea what it is. It is actually reacting to what we are doing.

David Fravor

Commander, US Navy; F/A-18 pilot and Black Aces squadron commander

2019 | Unidentified S1 Ep 1: The UFO Insiders

Pilots are screaming and everyone on the radio is screaming.

Kevin Day

Senior chief, US Navy; lead radar operator, *USS Princeton*

2021 | In Plain Sight, p 141

I kind of pull a nose to where he is going to be; he just rapidly accelerates beyond anything that I have ever seen, crosses my nose, and it's gone. And I'm like, "*woah*"…. The controller from the [USS] Princeton comes up right as we are doing all this and says, "Hey sir, you are not going to believe this. That thing is at your CAP [combat air patrol] point." You got something that can accelerate and disappear and then show up 60 miles away [> 3,600 mph]. Kind of in awe a little bit, because we don't have that.

David Fravor
Commander, US Navy; F/A-18 pilot and Black Aces squadron commander
2019 | Unidentified S1 Ep 1: The UFO Insiders

So your mind tries to make sense of it. I'm going to categorize this as maybe a helicopter or maybe a drone, and when it disappeared, I mean it was just...

Alex Dietrich
Lieutenant, US Navy; F/A-18 pilot
5/16/2021 | 60 Minutes

It was there...then it rifled out of sight in a split second. It was as if the object was shot out of a rifle. There was no gradual acceleration or spooling up period, it just shot out of sight immediately. I have never seen anything like it before or since. No human could have withstood that kind of acceleration.

Jim Slaight
Lieutenant commander, US Navy; weapons system officer
2021 | In Plain Sight, p 142

[It went] right back up to 28,000 feet.... At that point, you've got your other aircraft launching off the carrier, and all these other intercepts were happening. Before I knew it, I had these objects raining out of the sky. *Choo choo choo choo choo*, it was raining UFOs. I am telling you, it was the most humbling experience of my life.

Kevin Day
Senior chief, US Navy; lead radar operator, *USS Princeton*
2021 | Unidentified S1 Ep 2: Raining UFOs

The thing that stood out to me the most was how erratic it was behaving. And what I mean by erratic is that its changes in altitude, air speed, and aspect were just unlike things that I've ever encountered before flying against other air targets. It was just behaving in ways that aren't physically normal. That's what caught my eye. Because aircraft, whether they are manned or unmanned, still have to obey the laws of physics. They have to have some source of lift, some propulsion. The Tic Tac was not doing that. It was going from like 50,000 feet to, you know, 100 feet in like seconds, which is not possible.

Chad Underwood
Lieutenant, US Navy; F/A-18 pilot
2019 | In Plain Sight, p 145

This thing was going berserk, like making turns. It is incredible the amount of *g*-forces that it would have put on a human. It made a maneuver like they were chasing it straight on, it was going with them, then this thing stopped turning, just gone. In an instant. The [FLIR] video you see now, that's just a small snippet in the beginning of the whole video.

Jason Turner
Petty officer, *USS Princeton*
2021 | In Plain Sight, p 146

Nothing accelerates that fast.... I doubt that we have developed that technology.

David Fravor
Commander, US Navy; F/A-18 pilot and Black Aces squadron commander
10/6/2020 | The Phenomenon

There is something there measurable by multiple instruments, yet it seems to move in directions that are inconsistent with what we know of physics or science more broadly. That, to me, poses questions of tremendous interest.

Adam Schiff
US Congress (D), chair of the House Intelligence Committee
5/17/2021 | Congressional hearings

[Reading the classified UAP report as a senator], the hair stood up on the back of my neck.... [The pilots] know they saw something.
Bill Nelson
NASA administrator
6/25/2021 | The Washington Post

In 18 incidents, described in 21 reports, observers reported unusual UAP movement patterns or flight characteristics. Some UAP appeared to remain stationary in winds aloft, move against the wind, maneuver abruptly, or move at considerable speed, without discernible means of propulsion. In a small number of cases, military aircraft systems processed radio frequency (RF) energy associated with UAP sightings. The [UAP Task Force] holds a small amount of data that appear to show UAP demonstrating acceleration or a degree of signature management.
Office of the Director of National Intelligence
Preliminary Assessment: Unidentified Aerial Phenomena 2021
6/25/2021 | Report to Congress

Hypersonic vehicles that we work on today want to be above 50,000 feet [not down to sea level].... You don't see any exhaust plumes [in the FLIR video], and they would show up in this type of [infrared] image. The shape is wrong. The flight regime, the point in the sky it flies to is wrong. How it flies is wrong.
Steve Justice
Director, Advanced Systems Development at Skunkworks, Lockheed Martin
2019 | Unidentified S1 Ep 2: Raining UFOs

[Commenting on 2015 Go Fast video] If this were some type of aircraft with a conventional propulsion system, we would definitely see some type of heat signature [on the FLIR video]. Everything we know about propulsion systems is that they create an intense amount of heat.

Christopher Cooke
Lieutenant colonel, US Marines; pilot
2019 | Unidentified S1 Ep 4: UFO Fleet

The fact that [the 2015 GIMBAL UAP] was just getting himself on his wingtip [at 90 degrees], with no turn, while staying in the exact same point, isn't how aircraft work.
Ryan Graves
Lieutenant, US Navy; F/A-18 pilot
2019 | Unidentified S1 Ep 4: UFO Fleet

[Commenting on the 2015 GIMBAL video] It is definitely rotating, or changing angle of bank. It appears to have stopped moving quickly across the horizon. I have no idea. I have always been skeptical…but I have never seen anything remotely like what I saw today. I am a lot more convinced now that these vehicles do exist.
Christopher Cooke
Lieutenant colonel, US Marines; pilot
2019 | Unidentified S1 Ep 4: UFO Fleet

On a clear, sunny day in April 2014, two F/A-18s took off for an air combat training mission off the coast of Virginia. The jets, part of my Navy fighter squadron, climbed to an altitude of 12,000 and steered towards Warning Area W-72, an exclusive block of airspace ten miles east of Virginia Beach. All traffic into the training area goes through a single GPS point at a set altitude—almost like a doorway into a massive room where military jets can operate without running into other aircraft. Just at the moment the two jets crossed the threshold, one of the pilots saw a dark gray cube inside of a clear sphere—motionless against the wind, fixed directly at the entry point. The jets, only 100 feet apart, zipped past the object on either side. The pilots had come so dangerously close to something they couldn't identify that they terminated the training mission immediately and returned to base.

Ryan Graves
Lieutenant, US Navy; F/A-18 pilot
2/28/23 | Politico

As a pilot and former Air Force officer, I can definitely say that this craft [Phoenix Lights incident] did not resemble any man-made object I'd ever seen. And it was certainly not high-altitude flares [as stated by the Air Force], because flares don't fly in formation.

Fife Symington
Governor, Arizona
1997 | In Plain Sight p 119

My position both privately and publicly expressed over the last dozen years or more [about the 1980 Rendlesham forest incident at RAF Bentwaters], is that there are only two possibilities, either: a) An intrusion into our air space and a landing by unidentified craft took place at Rendlesham, as described. Or: b) The Deputy Commander of an operational, nuclear armed, US Air Force base in England, and a large number of his enlisted men, are lying. Either of these simply must be "of interest to the Ministry of Defence," which has been repeatedly denied, in precisely those terms.

Lord Hill-Norton
Admiral, UK Chief of the Defence Staff
10/22/1997 | UFOs: Generals ... p 173

[Tape recording during Rendlesham incident with other soldiers]

I see it, too.... It's back again.... It's coming this way.... There is no doubt about it.... This is weird.... It looks like an eye winking at you.... It almost burns your eyes.... He's coming towards us now.... [panic] Now we are observing what appears to be a beam coming down to the ground.... One object still hovering over Woodbridge base...beaming down.

Charles Halt
Lieutenant colonel, US Air Force, deputy base commander, RAF Bentwaters
12/28/1980 | UFOs: Generals ... p 170

I was the senior security officer in charge of Woodbridge base security [Rendlesham].... I held a top-secret US and NATO security clearance.... It maneuvered through the trees and shot off at an unbelievable rate of speed. It was gone in the blink of an eye. In my logbook, which I still have, I wrote "Speed Impossible." I subsequently learned that other personnel based at Bentwaters and Woodbridge, all trained observers, had witnessed this takeoff.

James Penniston
Sergeant, US Air Force
2010 | UFOs: Generals ... p 179

I spoke to former RAF radar operator Nigel Kerr [about Rendlesham]... for three or four sweeps, something did show up, directly over the base. But it faded away.... Arguably the most critical piece of evidence.... The Defence Intelligence Staff had assessed the radiation readings taken at the landing site and judged them to be "significantly higher than the average background"...about seven times what would have been expected for the area concerned.

Nick Pope
UK Ministry of Defense (Ret.)
2010 | UFOs: Generals ... p 171

Behind the scenes, high ranking Air Force officers are soberly concerned about the UFOs. But through official secrecy and ridicule, many citizens are led to believe the unknown flying objects are nonsense.... To hide the facts, the Air Force has silenced its personnel.

R.H. Hillenkoetter
Director of the Central Intelligence Agency, vice admiral, US Navy
2/28/1960 | The New York Times

If we persist in refusing to recognize the existence of the UFOs, we will end up, one fine day, by mistaking them for the guided missiles of an enemy—and the worst will be upon us.

L. M. Chassin
General NATO coordinator of Allied Air Service
1960 | US Air Force

No agency in this country or Russia is able to duplicate at this time the speeds and accelerations which radars and observers indicate the flying objects are able to achieve. There are signs that an intelligence directs these objects because of the way they fly. The way they change position in formations would indicate that their motion is directed.

Delmer Fahrney
Admiral, head of Navy guided-missile program
1/1/1957 | In Plain Sight p 47

Sightings of unexplained objects at great altitudes and traveling at high speeds in the vicinity of major U.S. defense installations are of such nature that they are not attributable to natural phenomena or known types of aerial vehicles.

H. Marshall Chadwell
Assistant director of the CIA, Scientific Intelligence
12/2/1952 | The New York Times

Probably what we saw [in 1952 over Washington, DC] was from somewhere else. Look, the Air Force is a very deadly being when it comes to intercepting an unknown. If it proves hostile, we are going to shoot it down. Other than that, no problem.

William Coleman
Colonel, US Air Force; public spokesman for Project Blue Book
10/6/2020 | The Phenomenon

[In 1952 over Washington, DC], I am convinced they are solid objects. I am convinced that they are probably from another planet or outer space somewhere. I have always felt that way since that night.

Albert M Chop
Press spokesman for Project Blue Book
10/6/2020 | The Phenomenon

[At an Air Force base in Germany 1952:] Unlike fighters, they would almost stop in their forward velocity and change 90 degrees, sometimes in their flight path…. We had practically all the fighters we could muster on the base up climbing as high as they could climb with guys that have binoculars with them…. They were round in shape and very metallic looking. And they would come over and do the same maneuvers that we make except everyone once in a while one of them goes "zip" [hand motion]. And you just can't do that in a fighter.

Gordon Cooper
NASA astronaut and US Air Force fighter pilot
1998 | The Phenomenon

They came in like this and went out like this [makes a *v*]. There would be no way to make a complete reversal or 90 degree turn at 12,000 miles [per hour] or greater without making the occupants juice on the wall. That kind of really shook us up…. Nothing could have gotten to that degree of scientific progress without some of the intermediate steps becoming public knowledge. We just knew that they were not from this planet.

William Nash
Pan American pilot, former fighter pilot
10/6/2020 | The Phenomenon

Since 1947 we have received and analyzed between 1,000 and 2,000 reports…. However, there have been a certain percentage of this volume of these reports, that have been made by credible observers of relatively incredible things. We can say that the recent sightings are in no way connected with any secret development by any department by the United States.

John Samford
Director of Intelligence, major general in the US Air Force
1952 | The Phenomenon

...not entirely impossible that the objects sighted may possibly be ships from another planet such as Mars.

John Samford
Director of Intelligence, major general US Air Force
1952 | UFOs: Generals ...

This [Evelyn and Paul Trent case] is one of the few UFO cases in which all factors investigated, geometric, psychological, and physical, appear to be consistent with the assertion that an extraordinary flying object, silvery, metallic, disc-shaped, tens of meters in diameter, and evidently artificial flew within sight of two witnesses.

Air Force UAP inquiry
Case 46: McKinville. Oregon
5/11/1950 | Condon Report

The [UAP] phenomenon reported is something real and not visionary or fictitious...extreme rates of climb, maneuverability (particularly in roll), and motion which must be considered evasive when sighted or contacted by friendly aircraft and radar...[that] lend belief to the possibility that some of the objects are controlled either manually, or remotely.

Nathan Twining
Commander of Air Materiel Command, lieutenant general in the US Air Force
9/23/1947 | US Air Force

I kept looking for their tails. They don't have any tails. I thought, *Well something is wrong with my eyes.* They seemed to flip and flash in the sun just like a mirror. I'd be glad to confirm it with my hands on a Bible because I did see it. Whether it has anything to do with our army or some foreign country, I don't know.

Kenneth Arnold
Pilot
1947 | The Phenomenon

All over the world. There have been sightings all over the world.

John Ratcliffe
Director of National Intelligence
3/22/2021 | The Guardian

Allies have seen these. China has created its own version of a UAP task force, so clearly a number of countries have seen objects in their airspace that they can't identify.

Scott Bray
Deputy director of Navy Intelligence
5/17/2022 | Congressional hearings

Both countries [China and Russia] have active UFO groups…. They certainly have had their own incidents over the years…. France has had an official UFO investigative group for decades. This is very much a global phenomenon.

Christopher Mellon
Deputy Assistant Secretary of Defense for Intelligence
5/30/2021 | The Joe Rogan Experience

For twenty-one years, from 1983 to 2004, I was the director of the French program to investigate and analyze unidentified aerospace phenomena…. The existence of UFOs is without question. UFOs seem to be "artificially controlled objects" and their physical characteristics can be measured by our detection systems—particularly radar. They display a physics seemingly far different from that which we employ in our most technologically advanced countries. Ground and on-board radar show that their performance greatly exceed[s] our best aeronautical and space capabilities. These capabilities include stationary and silent flights, accelerations and speeds defying the laws of inertia.

Jean-Jacques Velasco
Director of GEPAN; head of French UAP program
2010 | UFOs: Generals ... p 128

In 10 of the 11 cases [investigated], the conclusion was that the witnesses had witnessed a material phenomenon that could not be explained as a natural phenomenon or a human device. One of the conclusions of the total report is that behind the overall phenomenon there is a "flying machine...whose modes of sustenance and propulsion are beyond our knowledge."

National Security Agency
Declassified summary of GEPAN report, French government UAP office
1999 | Document

Hundreds of people [in 1989] saw a majestic triangular craft with a span of approximately 120 feet, powerful beaming spotlights, moving very slowly without making any significant noise, but, in several cases, accelerating to very high speeds. [In] the following days and months, many more sightings would follow.... On one occasion two F-16s registered changes in speed and altitude which were well outside the performance envelope of existing aircraft.

Wilfred De Brouwer
Deputy chief of staff, major general, Belgian Air Force
2010 | In Plain Sight, p 89

The crafts performed in ways not possible by known technology. They were able to remain stationary and hover, even in unusual positions such as vertical and/or banking at 45 degrees or more. They could fly at slow speeds and accelerate extremely fast, faster than any known aircraft, and they remained silent, or made only a very slight noise, even when hovering or accelerating.

Wilfred De Brouwer

Deputy chief of staff, major general, Belgian Air Force

2010 | UFOs: Generals ... p 35

On the morning of Number 2, 1982...I noticed...another "aircraft." It didn't have wings and it didn't have a tail, only a cockpit! It was an oval shape. What kind of airplane could that be?... I flew directly to a point along the trajectory of its elliptical course. It came toward me and flew right over me, on top of my aircraft, and stopped there, like a helicopter landing but much, much faster, breaking all the rules of aerodynamics. It was very close to my plane, only about 15 feet. I was astonished. I closed my eyes and I froze at this moment without reacting. There was no impact.... It then flew off in a flash.... One of the other pilots saw the whole thing.... Right after landing, all three of us filed detailed, independent written reports about the incident.

Julio Miguel Guerra

Captain, Portuguese Air Force

2010 | UFOs: Generals ... p 49

On April 11, 1980 at 7:15 am...the squad commander...ordered me to take off...to intercept the balloon before it got any closer to our base.... Zeroing in on the balloon...I shot a burst of sixty-four 30mm shells, which created a cone-shaped "wall of fire" that would normally obliterate anything in its path...but nothing happened. Then suddenly the object began to ascend very rapidly and head away from the base.... I initiated a chase...at a speed of 600 mph and the "balloon" remained about 1,600 feet in front of me...[up to] 36,000 feet. It came to a sudden stop and forced me to veer to the side.... It eluded my attack three times, each time at the very last moment. We reached an altitude of 63,000 feet and suddenly the thing stopped completely and remained stationary.... I got as close as about 300 feet from it. I was startled to see that the "balloon" was not a balloon at all. It was an object that measured about 35 feet in diameter…. It lacked all the typical components of aircraft. It had no wings, propulsion jets, exhausts, windows, antennae, and so forth. It had no visible propulsion system. At that moment, I realized this was not a spying device but a UFO, something totally unknown…. Suddenly, I was afraid.

Oscar Santa Maria Huertas
Commandant, Peruvian Air Force
2010 | UFOs: Generals … p 89

December 9, 1979 at around 9:15 am… The object [had] a precise contour, a gray metal color on the top and dark blue below, with no lights or portholes. It went about three meters from the ground, not stabilized, and then rose to the level of the trees [250 meters away], while continuously oscillating, then went down again slightly and stopped. It went up a little once again, always while oscillating; it tilted and accelerated quickly to reach a speed much higher than that of a Mirage III [French fighter jet capable of Mach 2], and disappeared.

Jean-Pierre Fartek
Captain, French Air Force
1979 | UFOs: Generals … p 124

An outstanding report: this [1976 Tehran] case is a classic which meets all the criteria necessary for a valid study of the UFO phenomenon. The object was seen by multiple witnesses from different locations…and viewpoints. The credibility of many of the witnesses was high (an Air Force General, qualified aircrews and experienced tower operators). Visual sightings were confirmed by radar. Similar electromagnetic effects were reported by three separate aircraft. There were physiological effects on some crew members (i.e., loss of night vision due to the brightness of the object). An inordinate amount of maneuverability was displayed by the UFOs.

Roland Evans
Major colonel, Defense Intelligence Agency
10/12/1976 | UFOs: Generals … p 150

At about 11 pm on the evening of September 18, 1976, citizens were frightened by the circling of an unknown object over Tehran at a low altitude. It looked similar to a star, but bigger and brighter.... And then I saw it. It was flashing with intense red, green, orange, and blue lights so bright I was not able to see its body.... I approached, and I got close to it, maybe 70 miles or so in a climb situation. All of a sudden, it jumped about 10 degrees to the right, in an instant! [6.7 miles]. Ten degrees.... And then it jumped 10 degrees, and then again.... We now had a good [radar] return on the screen, and it was at 27 miles.... At this moment, I thought this was my chance to fire at it. But it—whatever it was—was close to me, my weapons jammed and my radio communications were garbled. We got closer, to 25 miles at our twelve o'clock position. All of a sudden it jumped back to 27 miles in an instant.... I was really scared.... I attempted to fire, and looked at the panel to confirm my selection of the missile. Suddenly, nothing was working. The weapons control panel was out, and I lost all the instruments, and the radio. The indicator dials were spinning around randomly, and the instruments were fluctuating...[the UAP] started circling around us.

Parviz Jafari
General, Iranian Air Force
2010 | UFOs: Generals ... p 88

I'm glad the Pentagon is finally releasing this footage, but it only scratches the surface of research and materials available.

Harry Reid
US senator (D); Senate majority leader
4/27/2020 | Twitter

I am saying most of [the evidence] hasn't seen the light of day.

Harry Reid
US senator (D); Senate majority leader
5/16/2021 | The Phenomenon

I actually wanted to get this information out and declassify it before I left office but we weren't able to get it down into an unclassified format that we were able to talk about quickly enough.

John Ratcliffe
Director of National Intelligence
3/22/2021 | Fox News

If UAP do indeed represent a potential threat to our security, then the capabilities, systems, processes, and sources we use to observe, record, study or analyze these phenomena need to be classified at appropriate levels. We do not want potential adversaries to know exactly what we're able to see or understand or how we come to the conclusions we make. Therefore public disclosures must be carefully considered on a case by case basis.

Scott Bray
Deputy director of Navy Intelligence
5/17/2022 | Congressional hearings

Finally my biggest failure of 2014, once again not securing the disclosure of UFO files.

John Podesta
Chief of staff to President Bill Clinton
2/13/2015 | Twitter

I did attempt to discover if there were any secret government documents that reveal things, and if there were, they were concealed from me, too. I wouldn't be the first president that underlings had lied to or career bureaucrats have waited out. There may be some career person sitting around somewhere hiding these dark secrets even from elected presidents, but if so, they successfully eluded me and I am almost embarrassed to tell you I did try to find out.

Bill Clinton
US president (D)
2014 | The Phenomenon

At some point, the information about "alien" stuff and true US national defence information crosses paths. Patriots with clearances do not want to be traitors to their country or their way of life. For instance, if I told you the exact electromagnetic signature of a high-match UFO that US sensors search for, but don't attack, and you put it in a book, the Soviets/Chinese would manufacture a bomber with sigint/elint countermeasure equipment that generated that exact signature.

Bob Fish
Defense communications intelligence
2021 | In Plain Sight, p 103

If there is some recovered debris say, it is so deeply buried and squirreled away that it's outside of those normal oversight processes, and that's why there is a problem in this area.

Christopher Mellon
Deputy assistant secretary of defense for Intelligence
5/16/2021 | The Phenomenon

After looking into this, I came to the conclusion that there were reports—some were substantive, some not so substantive—that there were actual [UAP] materials that the government and the private sector had in their possession.... It is extremely important that information about the discovery of physical materials or retrieved craft come out.

Harry Reid
US senator (D); Senate majority leader
7/23/2020 | The New York Times

[Tucker Carlson]: Do you think the US government has debris from a UFO right now?

[Elizondo]: Aaah, simply put, yes.

Luis Elizondo
Director AATIP; head of Pentagon UAP program
5/1/2019 | In Plain Sight, p. 244

Luis Elizondo's very brief answer to Tucker Carlson's question about whether the US government is in possession of recovered, crashed, and landed UFO technology hardware is 1,000% accurate. My national security NDAs prevent me from adding any further comment to this.

Dr. Eric Davis
Astrophysicist; consultant to AATIP, Pentagon UAP study program
6/2/2019 | In Plain Sight, p. 245

[Coulthart]: Are you able to confirm to me that the US has been trying to develop recovered alien technology?

[Kobitz]: Yes, I can say that's so.

Nat Kobitz
Director of US Navy Science and Technology Development
2020 | In Plain Sight, p. 282

I will tell you, I have never said this before, but I have been told by multiple people who have credentials and access, that there is some truth to these stories [about Roswell]. So I don't discount this when people say this, I have had people who had substantial scientific or military credentials, that they believe it is true. So I encourage people on the Hill to pursue it.

Christopher Mellon
Deputy assistant secretary of defense for Intelligence
5/30/2021 | The Joe Rogan Experience

I won't talk to you about what I know about [Roswell], but it's very interesting.... [Asked by his son, Donald Trump, Jr., to declassify it] Well, I'll have to think about that one.

Donald Trump
US president (R)
6/19/2020 | NBC News

There was so much [debris at Roswell]. It was scattered over such a vast area [twelve football fields]. We found a piece of metal, about a foot and a half or two feet wide, about two to three feet long, felt like it had nothing in your hands. It wasn't any thicker than the foil out of a pack of cigarettes. The thing that got me is that you couldn't even bend it, you couldn't dent it, even a sledge hammer would bounce off of it.... All I could do was keep my mouth shut. Being an intelligence officer, I was familiar with every, just about all the materials used in aircraft, and in air travel, this was nothing like that. It was not anything from this earth, that I am quite sure of.

Jesse Marcel

Major, US Air Force; chief intelligence officer, Roswell Army Air Field

[1993] | The Phenomenon

Mr. Davis, who now works for Aerospace Corporation, a defense contractor, said he gave a classified briefing to a Defense Department agency as recently as March about retrievals from "off-world vehicles not made on this earth." Mr. Davis said he also gave classified briefings on retrievals of unexplained objects to staff members of the Senate Armed Services Committee on Oct. 21, 2019, and to staff members of the Senate Intelligence Committee two days later.

The New York Times

"No Longer in Shadows, Pentagon's U.F.O. Unit Will Make Some Findings Public"

7/23/2020 | The New York Times

Even before this "whistleblower" legislation was signed into law, credible individuals were providing Congress information alleging that the US government has recovered extraterrestrial technology. This process began in 2019 when I brought astrophysicist Dr. Eric Davis to Capitol

Hill to meet with staff from the Senate Intelligence and Armed Services committees. Dr. Davis, author of the famous Wilson-Davis memo, provided specific information lending credence to sensational reports that an official US government program is actively seeking to exploit recovered technology that was fashioned by some other species or perhaps advanced AI machines.

Christopher Mellon
Deputy assistant secretary of defense for Intelligence
12/24/2022 | Unprecedented UAP Legislation

We have crash retrievals and they have been analysed, and unfortunately our laboratory diagnostic technologies and our material sciences and the understanding of physics that we had were not advanced enough to be able to make heads or tails of what it is, of what they had their hands on.

[Editor's note: Mr. Davis retains his security clearance and government contractor employment despite making this public claim.]

Dr. Eric Davis
Astrophysicist; consultant to AATIP, Pentagon UAP study program
In Plain Sight, p 155

[Rogan]: [What about the] possibility that we have obtained this extraterrestrial craft and are in the process of trying to back engineer it?

Mellon]: That's a really ticklish question for me and awkward. And if I were to say "Yep, it's true" nobody would believe me. If I really knew, I couldn't say yes. And it's hard to give good answers to that question. I think it's plausible. I don't think people should rule that out. There's enough information to say that may have happened. We may have recovered some debris.... It would be so deeply squirreled away you wouldn't be able to bring in the best scientists, you wouldn't be able to bring in world class scientists, you would have a few people available in some aerospace company and they would be hamstrung in their ability to test and examine the material and so forth. It would just be locked away somewhere.

Christopher Mellon
Deputy assistant secretary of defense for Intelligence
5/30/2021 | The Joe Rogan Experience

I talk over the following weeks with other anonymous insiders. To protect their identities, I cannot reveal much of the astonishing detail of what they told me but I am left in no doubt that they all assert that the US military, almost certainly the US Air Force, is in possession of retrieved non-terrestrial—alien—technology. Intriguingly, what I am told matches the claims made in the Admiral Wilson memo, that a private aerospace company now exercises control over this alien technology.

Ross Coulthart
Investigative journalist; author of *In Plain Sight*
2021 | In Plain Sight, p 286

I was told for decades that Lockheed had some of these retrieved materials. And I tried to get, as I recall, a classified approval by the Pentagon to have me go look at the stuff. They would not approve that. I don't know what all the numbers were, what kind of classification it was, but they would not give that to me. That's why I wanted AATIP [to get Special-Access Program status] to take a look at it. But they wouldn't give me the clearance.

Harry Reid
US senator (D), Senate majority leader
5/1/2021 | The New Yorker

MORE FROM THE AUTHOR

For readers captivated by the themes explored in this book, Tyler Gilreath's previous works offer a deeper exploration of biblical cosmic conflict, supernatural rebellion, and divine mysteries that have shaped human history.

Gospel Over Gods provides a comprehensive, chronological study of the supernatural war throughout the Bible. Gilreath delves into the origins of the Nephilim giants, tracing their lineage to the fall of the sons of God in Genesis 6:1–4. This rebellion not only led to the corruption of humanity, but also introduced the giants, who play a central role in the spiritual conflict of the Old Testament. Additionally, *Gospel Over Gods* examines the Tower of Babel rebellion, uncovering how this pivotal event served as the backdrop for the rise of the "gods" of the Old Testament—spiritual entities who sought to challenge Yahweh's rule over the nations. Gilreath meticulously traces these events to reveal the enduring spiritual war from creation to Christ's ultimate victory.

In *Gate of the Gods*, Gilreath presents a revelatory examination of the book of Revelation and its profound connections to ancient Babylon. He uncovers the spiritual and historical significance of Babylon, illustrating how this ancient city plays a fundamental role in biblical prophecy. By linking Babylon to the apocalyptic visions of Revelation, *Gate of the Gods* reveals how its legacy of rebellion against God foreshadows the final battle in the end times. Gilreath sheds light on Babylon's enduring influence and its part in the unfolding of the end-time prophecies.

Both *Gospel Over Gods* and *Gate of the Gods* equip readers with a biblically grounded understanding of the supernatural worldview found in Scripture. Tyler Gilreath's works provide essential insight for those seeking to grasp the spiritual warfare that defines both the ancient and present worlds, offering a unique and thought-provoking perspective on the ongoing cosmic struggle. A brief preview of *Gate of the Gods* has been included to give readers a flavor of this work.

GATE OF THE GODS PREVIEW

t is entirely understandable why Rome gets so much attention in Revelation; the seven churches of Asia Minor lived under Roman rule. Although John never names Rome anywhere in the book, it's universally believed that John uses "Babylon" (14:6; 16:19; 17:4; 18:2, 10, 21) as a *cryptic* cipher or substitute for Rome. This conflation makes a lot of sense. Babylon and King Nebuchadnezzar leveled Jerusalem, destroyed the temple, and carried its people into exile just five hundred years before Rome did it to Israel in AD 70. So, Babylon's past actions against the Jewish community became *archetypal* to Rome's cruelty against God's people in the first century. This is well documented in many contemporary and later Jewish texts (see 2 Baruch 11:1; 33:2; 67:7; 79:1; Sibylline Oracles 5:140–143, 158–61, 434; 1 Peter 5:13; Midrash Rabbah Leviticus 6:6; Midrash Rabbah Song of Songs 1:6, 4; cf. 1Q Pesher Habakkuk II, 11–12 [a commentary on Habakkuk from the Dead Sea Scrolls]; Babylonian Talmud, Sanhedrin 21b [A passage from the Tractate Sanhedrin in the Babylonian Talmud]).[115] That John and the early church saw Rome as a *latter-day* Babylon is indisputable.

However, what if I told you that when John discusses Babylon in the book of Revelation, *OT Babylon* was fundamentally on his mind? What if I told you John saw Rome as the latest national *string puppet* in a long line of marionettes manipulated by the puppeteering angels from the Tower of Babel? The shocking content in this book will prove precisely that, and will shatter your paradigm concerning Babylon's identity in the book of Revelation.

In my book, *Gospel Over Gods*, I discuss in great detail how the Tower of Babel event in Deuteronomy 32:8 explains the origins of national gods. At Babel, God divorced the nations and allotted them to angelic sons of God (Deuteronomy 32:8–9). Note the following table.

Deuteronomy 32:8 (English Standard Version)	Deuteronomy 32:8 (Lexham English Septuagint)	Deuteronomy 32:8 (The Message)
"When the Most High gave to the nations their inheritance, when he divided mankind, he fixed the borders of the peoples according to the number of the *sons of God.*"	"When the Most High distributed nations as he scattered the descendants of Adam, he set up boundaries for the nations according to the number of the *angels of God.*"	"When the High God gave the nations their stake, gave them their place on Earth, He put each of the peoples within boundaries under the care of *divine guardians.*"

These *gods* did not walk according to their divine instructions, but led the nations into chaos and utter darkness, just as Psalm 82 explains:

God stands in the divine assembly; he administers judgment in the midst of *the* gods. "How long will you judge unjustly and show favoritism to the wicked? *Selah.* Judge *on behalf of the* helpless and *the* orphan; provide justice *to the* afflicted and *the* poor. Rescue *the* helpless and *the* needy; deliver *them* from the hand of *the* wicked." They do not know or consider. They go about in the darkness, *so that* all *the* foundations of *the* earth are shaken. I have said, "You *are* gods, and sons of the Most High, all of you. However, you will die like men, and you will fall like one of the princes." Rise up, O God, judge the earth, because you shall inherit all the nations." (Psalm 82, LEB)

Psalm 82 is a preview into the courtroom of Heaven. Asaph, the psalmist, describes a scene where the gods of the nations are judged for their crimes; they have led the nations astray, away from Yahweh's light, deep into the darkness, and now they must die like men.

How does all of this relate to Babylon? The linguistic leap from Babel to Babylon is obvious; the two are phonetically linked. However, more than that, they are *historically* linked. To understand how, we need to revisit ancient history.

The Bible credits Nimrod (the builder of the Tower of Babel) with building the ancient cities of Mesopotamia (Genesis 10:10–11). Mesopotamia was a fertile region between the Tigris and Euphrates. Nimrod built Babel, Erech, Akkad, and Calneh (which literally means "the place of Anu," one of the three chief gods of Sumerian religion). These cities were in southern Mesopotamia in the region of Shinar, commonly known as Sumer. The people inhabiting Sumer were known as the Sumerians. Scripture also credits Nimrod with the early development of the northern most part of Mesopotamia called Ashur, which eventually became Assyria.

The point is, the entirety of Mesopotamia can be traced back to Nimrod, the leading architect behind the Tower of Babel.

Over the next several thousand years, Mesopotamia split into two sections, Babylon and Assyria. These lands were ruled by various influential dynasties, including that of Hammurabi, the only Babylonian leader to gain control over all of Mesopotamia.[116] Babylonia in the south spanned twenty-three thousand square miles (about the size of West Virginia). This region coincides mostly with the area occupied by the Sumerians in the third millennium.[117] In the north was Assyria, which spanned seventy-five thousand square miles (a little smaller than the state of Nebraska).[118]

Babylon was the capital city of Babylonia and was in the same neighborhood as the infamous and much older Tower of Babel. *Babylon's writings, religion, and deities are therefore inseparable from the Babel event.* That John sees Old Testament Babylon as the harbinger of cosmic evil in Revelation is not figurative.

Chaos and Evil Hatched from Babylon

In *Gate of the Gods*, readers will discover many unique connections to Old Testament Babylon and recover *John's hidden Babylonian framework* that lies within. These subtle and sometimes drastic pen strokes lead readers *far beyond the time of Rome*, back to Babylon, Babel, and the ancient gods of the primeval world.

ENDNOTES

1   United States. Congress. House. Committee on Oversight and Accountability. Subcommittee on National Security, the Border, and Foreign Affairs. Unidentified Anomalous Phenomena: Implications on National Security, Public Safety, and Government Transparency: Hearing before the Subcommittee on National Security, the Border, and Foreign Affairs of the Committee on Oversight and Accountability, House of Representatives, One Hundred Eighteenth Congress, First Session, July 26, 2023. Washington: U.S. Government Publishing Office, 2023.

2   Ibid.

3   Ibid.

4   Ibid.

5   Ibid.

6   Ibid.

7   Ibid.

8   Ibid.

9   Ibid.

10 Ibid.

11 Ibid.

12 Ibid.

13 Ibid

14 Ibid

15 Ibid

16 "To George Washington from the American Philosophical Society, 12 December 1796," Founders Online, National Archives, https://founders.archives.gov/documents/Washington/05-21-02-0152. [Original source: *The Papers of George Washington*, Presidential Series, vol. 21, 22 September 1796–3 March 1797, ed. Adrina Garbooshian-Huggins. Charlottesville: University of Virginia Press, 2020, pp. 354–355.]

17 George Washington, "Letter to David Rittenhouse." American Revolution Institute. Accessed August 5, 2024. https://www.americanrevolutioninstitute.org/masterpieces-in-detail/george-washington-letter-to-david-rittenhouse/.

18 Benjamin Rush, "An Eulogium, Intended to Perpetuate the Memory of David Rittenhouse, Late President of the American Philosophical Society, Delivered before the Society in the First Presbyterian Church, in High-street, Philadelphia, on the 17th Dec. 1796." Accessed August 8, 2024. https://ota.bodleian.ox.ac.uk/repository/xmlui/bitstream/handle/20.500.12024/N23511/N23511.html?sequence=5&isAllowed=y.

19 Ibid.

20 Ibid.

21 Ibid.

22 Ibid.

23 Charles Francis Adams (John Adams' grandson), *The Works of John Adams, Second President of the United States: With a Life of the Author, Notes and Illustrations* 10 vols (Boston: Little, Brown & Co., 1856). Vol. 2, p. 13.

24 Ibid., p. 14.

25 Ibid.

26 Robert D. Gingrich, *Faith & Freedom: The Founding Fathers in Their Own Words* (Uhrichsville, OH: Barbour Books, 2012).

27 Ibid.

28 *The Papers of George Washington.* Digital edition (Charlottesville: University of Virginia Press, Rotunda). 2008.

29 Charles Francis Adams, *The Works of John Adams.* Vol. 2, p. 18.

30 Benjamin Franklin, "Articles of Belief and Acts of Religion, 20 November 1728." Autograph manuscript, Library of Congress. Also transcript, Library of Congress. Mentioned in *The Autobiography of Benjamin Franklin.* Accessed September 30, 2024. https://founders.archives.gov/documents/Franklin/01-01-02-0002.

31 David A. Weintraub, *Religions and Extraterrestrial Life: How Will We Deal with It?* (Springer Praxis Books, Springer International Publishing). pp. 88–89, Kindle edition.

32 Gingrich, *Faith & Freedom.*

33 "Founding Fathers: The Essential Guide to the Men Who Made America" *Encyclopaedia Britannica* (Turner Publishing Co.). pp. 116–117. Kindle edition.

34 Ibid., pp. 120–121.

35 William Dunbar and Thomas Jefferson, "Description of a Singular Phenomenon Seen at Baton Rouge." *Transactions of the American Philosophical Society*, vol. 6, 1809, p. 25. American Philosophical Society. Accessed June 6, 2024. https://www.jstor.org/stable/1004759.

36 Ibid.

37 John Page and David Rittenhouse, "A Letter to David Rittenhouse, Esq. from John Page, Esq. From David Rittenhouse, Esq. to John Page, Esq. Concerning a Remarkable Meteor Seen in Virginia and Pennsylvania." Transactions of the American Philosophical Society, vol. 2, 1786, pp. 173–176. American Philosophical Society. Accessed October 6, 2024. https://www.jstor.org/stable/1005176.

38 Dunbar and Jefferson, "Description of a Singular Phenomenon," p. 25.

39 Ibid.

40 Ibid.

41 Ibid.

42 Thomas Jefferson, "An Atmospheric Phenomenon." Monticello, accessed October 6, 2024. https://www.monticello.org/research-education/for-scholars/papers-of-thomas-jefferson/featured-letters/an-atmospheric-phenomenon/.

43 Thomas Jefferson, "Letter to John Adams. 1 June 1812." Founders Online, National Archives. Accessed October 7, 2024. https://founders.archives.gov/?q=

Author%3A%22Jefferson%2C%20Thomas%22%20Recipient%3A%22Adams
%2C%20John%22%20Period%3A%22post-Madison%20Presidency%22&s
=1521311113&r=7.

44 "Founding Fathers: The Essential Guide to the Men Who Made America," *Encyclopaedia Britannica*. p. 134.

45 Ibid.

46 From "Memo to George Marshall from FDR, 27 February 1942," available at Majestic Documents, https://majesticdocuments.com/pdf/fdr.pdf. Accessed August 8, 2024. Ryan S. Wood, *Majic Eyes Only: Earth's Encounters with Extraterrestrial Technology* (Wood Enterprises) p. 81, Kindle edition.

47 From "George C. Marshall to Franklin D. Roosevelt, 5 March 1942," available at Majestic Documents, https://majesticdocuments.com/pdf/marshall-fdr-march1942. pdf. Accessed on August 8, 2024. Ryan S. Wood, *Majic Eyes Only: Earth's Encounters with Extraterrestrial Technology* (Wood Enterprises). pp. 22–23, Kindle Edition.

48 "Franklin D. Roosevelt Memo on Non-Terrestrial Science and Technology, 22 February 1944." Accessed August 8, 2024, https://majesticdocuments.com/pdf/ fdr_22feb44.pdf.

49 Larry Holcombe, *The Presidents and UFOs: A Secret History from FDR to Obama* (St. Martin's Publishing Group). pp. 55–57, Kindle edition.

50 Ibid.

51 Chris Bledsoe, *UFO of GOD: The Extraordinary True Story of Chris Bledsoe* (David Broadwell). pp. 53–88, Kindle edition.

52 Ibid.

53 John F. Kennedy, "John F. Kennedy to Director, CIA, June 1961." Majestic Documents. Accessed August 10, 2024. https://majesticdocuments.com/pdf/kennedy_cia.pdf.

54 "Document Release: JFK Assassination Records – 104-10306-10025." National Archives, 2023. Accessed August 12, 2024. https://www.archives.gov/files/research /jfk/releases/2023/104-10306-10025.pdf.

55 John F. Kennedy, "John F. Kennedy to CIA, November 1961." Majestic Documents, Accessed August 03, 2024. https://majesticdocuments.com/pdf/kennedy_cia.pdf.

56 Holcombe, *The Presidents and UFOs*, p. 191.

57 Ryan S. Wood, *Majic Eyes Only: Earth's Encounters with Extraterrestrial Technology* (Wood Enterprises). pp. 368–369, Kindle edition.

58 M. Berger, "Jimmy Carter's Space Policy and the Saving of the Space Shuttle." *The Hill*. February 24, 2023. https://thehill.com/opinion/technology/3882188-jimmy -carters-space-policy-and-the-saving-of-the-space-shuttle/.

59 Wil S. Hylton, "The Gospel According to Jimmy." *GQ*. January 2006.

60 R. Dolan, "UAP Crash Retrievals, Bodies, & Secrecy," *Richard Dolan Show w/Michael Schratt*. YouTube video. https://youtu.be/_8GJwpRbXNw.

61 Ronald Reagan, "Address to the 42d Session of the United Nations General Assembly in New York, New York." Ronald Reagan Presidential Library & Museum, September 21, 1987. Accessed August 16, 2024. https://www.reaganlibrary.gov/archives /speech/address-42d-session-united-nations-general-assembly-new-york-new-york.

62 Bill Clinton, in *The Phenomenon*, a 2014 film directed by. James Fox (1091 Media).

63 President Bill Clinton and James Patterson talk about aliens and advertising on *LIVE with Kelly and Mark,* June 11, 2018YouTube video is available at https://youtu.be /Y4Pr9Zjxja0.

64 Holcombe, *The Presidents and UFOs,* p. 231).

65 "USG Has More Data." UAP Guide. Accessed August 26, 2024. https://www.uap .guide/quotes/USG-has-more-data. Accessed August 26, 2024.

66 Barack Obama, *Late Late Show with James Corden.* May 19, 2021. Available at https://www.youtube.com/watch?v=xp6Ph5iTIgc.

67 "Trump Says He's Heard 'Very Interesting' Things About Roswell." NBC News. Accessed June 17, 2024. https://www.nbcnews.com/politics/donald-trump/trump -says-he-s-heard-very-interesting-things-about-roswell-n1231521.

68 Aaron Reich, "Former Israeli Space Security Chief Says Aliens Exist, Humanity Not Ready." *Jerusalem Post,* December 5, 2020. Accessed February 3, 2024. https://www. jpost.com/omg/former-israeli-space-security-chief-says-aliens-exist-humanity-not -ready-651405.

69 "Donald Trump's UFO Admission Raises Eyebrows." *Newsweek.* Accessed August 26, 2024.https://www.newsweek.com/donald-trumps-ufo-admission-raises-eyebrows -1913016. Accessed August 26, 2024.

70 National Archives. "Presidential Libraries: Gerald R. Ford—Box D9, Folder 'Ford Congressional Papers: Press Secretary and Speech File'." Gerald R. Ford Presidential Library. Accessed August 16, 2024. https://s3.amazonaws.com/NARAprodstorage/lz /presidential-libraries/ford/grf-0054/642076/4525586.pdf.

71 Ibid.

72 Holcombe, *The Presidents and UFOs,* p. 177.

73 Paul Thigpen, *Extraterrestrial Intelligence and the Catholic Faith: Are We Alone in the Universe with God and the Angels?* (Ashland, OH: TAN Books, 2022).

74 Ted F. Peters, Martinez Hewlett, et al., *Astrotheology: Science and Theology Meet Extra-terrestrial Life* (Eugene, OR: Cascade Books, 2018).

75 Ibid.

76 Weintraub, *Religions and Extraterrestrial Life,* pp. 77–78.

77 Ibid.

78 Ibid.

79 OP: *Ordo Praedicatorum,* Latin for the "Order of Preachers," also known as the "Dominican Order."

80 Peters, Hewlett, et al., *Astrotheology.*

81 Ibid.

82 Paul Thigpen, "Extraterrestrial Intelligence and the Catholic Faith: A Brief History of an Ancient Conversation," March 1, 2024. Society of Catholic Scientists, https:// catholicscientists.org/articles/extraterrestrial-intelligence-and-the-catholic-faith-a -brief-history-of-an-ancient-conversation/.

83 Peters, Hewlett, et al., Astrotheology.

84 Yves Congar, "Has God Peopled the Stars?" Appendix 2 in *The Wide World My Parish: Salvation and Its Problems,* trans. Donald Attwater (Baltimore: Helicon Press,

1961), 184–96; available online at https://archive.org/details/thewideworldmyparish/page/n195/mode/2up.

85 Exotheology is the theological study of extraterrestrial life and its implications for religious beliefs, including salvation, creation, and divine purpose.

86 Astrotheology is the study of how celestial bodies (stars, planets, and cosmic phenomena) influence religious beliefs, myths, and rituals throughout history.

87 Paul Thigpen, *Extraterrestrial Intelligence and the Catholic Faith: Are We Alone in the Universe with God and the Angels?* (Ashland, OH: TAN Books, 2022).

88 Peters, Hewlett, et al., *Astrotheology.*

89 *The Holy Bible with Deuterocanon/Apocrypha* (M. P. Johnson, 2020), Judges 5:20–23.

90 Moed Katan, *The Babylonian Talmud: Moed Katan.* Translated by Rabbi Dr. I. Epstein (Soncino Press, 1938). https://halakhah.com/pdf/moed/Moed_Katan.pdf.

91 Whitley Strieber, *Them* (Walker & Collier, Inc.). p. 86–98, Kindle edition.

92 Ibid., p. 100–112.

93 Ibid., p. 114–124.

94 Ibid., p. 126–144.

95 Kathleen Marden and Denise Stoner, "The Marden-Stoner Study on Commonalities Among UFO Abduction Experiencers." Kathleen Marden, 2012. Accessed August 1, 2024. https://www.kathleen-marden.com/commonalities-study-on-ufo-abduction-experiencers.php.

96 Ibid.

97 Ibid.

98 Federal Bureau of Investigation, *The Vault: FBI Records,* "UFO Part 1 of 16.". Accessed August 16, 2023. https://vault.fbi.gov/UFO/UFO%20Part%201%20of%2016/view.

99 Ibid.

100 Luis Elizondo *Imminent: Inside the Pentagon's Hunt for UFOs: The Former Head of the Program Responsible for Investigating UAPs Reveals Profound Secrets* (HarperCollins). pp. 84–85, Kindle edition.

101 Ibid.

102 Thigpen, *Extraterrestrial Intelligence and the Catholic Faith: Are We Alone* .

103 Congar, "Has God Peopled the Stars?".

104 Tim Lomas, Brendan Case, & Michael P. Masters, "The Cryptoterrestrial Hypothesis: A Case for Scientific Openness to a Concealed Earthly Explanation for Unidentified Anomalous Phenomena." *Philosophy and Cosmology*, Volume 33.

105 Richard Dolan and Bryce Zabel. *A.D. After Disclosure: When the Government Finally Reveals the Truth About Alien Contact* (Red Wheel Weiser, 2012). Kindle edition.

106 Aaron Reich, "Former Israeli Space Security Chief Says Aliens Exist, Humanity Not Ready."

107 James Lacatski, Colm Kelleher, and George Knapp, *Inside the US Government Covert UFO Program: Initial Revelations* (RTMA LLC: Henderson, NV). p. 86, Kindle edition.

108 Benjamin Franklin, "From Benjamin Franklin: Convention Speech Proposing

Prayers (unpublished), June 28, 1787." *The Papers of Benjamin Franklin*. Accessed October 9, 2024. https://franklinpapers.org/framedVolumes.jsp?vol=45&page=077.

109 Ibid.

110 Ibid.

111 Ibid.

112 Ibid.

113 "President George Washington's First Inaugural Address." National Archives, n.d., Accessed October 3, 2024. https://www.archives.gov/milestone-documents/president -george-washingtons-first-inaugural-speech.

114 Abraham Lincoln, "Speech at Edwardsville, IL, 11 September 1858," *Collected Works of Abraham Lincoln*, vol. 3. https://quod.lib.umich.edu/l/lincoln/lincoln3 /1:13?rgn=div1;view=fulltext.

115 G. K. Beale and Sean M McDonough, "Revelation," in *Commentary on the New Testament Use of the Old Testament* (Grand Rapids, MI; Nottingham, UK: Baker Academic; Apollos, 2007), p. 1132.

116 Tammi J. Schneider, *An Introduction to Ancient Mesopotamian Religion* (Grand Rapids, MI; Cambridge, UK: Eerdmans Publishing Company, 2011). p. 26.

117 Ibid.

118 Morris Jastrow Jr., *The Religion of Babylonia and Assyria* (Boston, MA: Ginn & Co. Publishers, 1898), p. 26.

www.ingramcontent.com/pod-product-compliance
Lightning Source LLC
Jackson TN
JSHW032104200425
82984JS00007B/21